The Way We Lived Then

Recollections from Four Centuries
of Family Life

D1497021

The Way We Lived Then

———

Recollections from Four Centuries
of Family Life

———

Compiled by
Edward Armitage

with illustrations by
Peter Askem

Robson Books

First published in Great Britain in 2001 by Robson Books, 10 Blenheim Court, Brewery Road, London N7 9NY

A member of the Chrysalis Group plc

Copyright © 2001 Edward Armitage

The right of Edward Armitage to be identified as the author of this work has been asserted by him in accordance with the Copyright, Designs and Patents Act 1988.

The copyright holders of the individual extracts retain their copyright. See the acknowledgements page for a full listing.

The author and the publishers have made every reasonable effort to contact all copyright holders. Any errors that may have occurred are inadvertent and anyone who for any reason has not been contacted is invited to write to the publishers so that a full acknowledgement may be made in subsequent editions of this work.

British Library Cataloguing in Publication Data
A catalogue record for this title is available from the British Library.

ISBN 86105 389 4

Book Design by Robert Crocker
Typeset by SX Composing DTP, Rayleigh, Essex
Printed by Butler & Tanner Ltd., London and Frome

941
———
1405134

Contents

Acknowledgements

'The Insularity of Village Life' and 'The School Inspector' are extracts from *a Victorian Village* by Ralph Whitlock. Reprinted by permission of Laurence Pollinger Ltd and the estate of Ralph Whitlock.

'The Family Pig' and 'Houses in the late Nineteenth Century' are extracts from *Lark Rise* by Flora Thompson. Reprinted by permission of Oxford University Press.

'Earth Closets' is reproduced from *A Cornish Childhood* by A. L. Rowse. Reprinted by permission of Dr. A.L. Rowse.

'The Village Festival' and 'Sunday Chapel' are extracts from *Bright Boots* by Fred Gresswell. Reprinted by permission of the Gresswell family.

'The Fire' and 'Goody' are extracts of *To School Through the Fields* by Alice Taylor. Reprinted by permission of Mount Eagle Publications Ltd.

'The Workhouse' is reproduced from *Cider with Rosie* by Laurie Lee, published by Hogarth Press. Reprinted by permission of The Random House Group Ltd.

'Health' and 'Thrift' are extracts from *A Yeoman Farmer's Son* by H. St. G. Cramp. Reprinted by permission of John Murray (Publishers) Ltd.

'Pre-nuptial Agreements in 1594', 'Country-house Entertaining' and 'Ceremony at Mealtimes' are extracts from *A Country House Companion* by Mark Girouard. Reprinted by permission of Curtis Brown on behalf of Mark Girouard.

'Country-houses', 'Stage Coach', 'London's Services', 'The New Towns', 'The Mines and Child Labour' and 'Boxing' are extracts from *English Saga 1840-1940* by Sir Arthur Bryant, published by Collins. Reprinted by permission of David Higham Associates.

'London in 1660' and 'The Great Fire' are extracts from *Wren's London* by Eric de Mare. Reprinted by permission of The Folio Society Ltd.

'The Industrial Revolution', 'London in 1800' and 'Blockading French Ports' are extracts from *Years of Victory 1802-1812* by Sir Arthur Bryant, published by Collins. Reprinted by permission of David Higham Associates.

'Victorian Living Conditions', 'The Means Test', 'The Hygiene Inspection' and 'Corporal Punishment' are extracts from *On the Pig's Back* by Bill Naughton. Reprinted by permission of Oxford University Press.

'Suffragettes' and 'The Knocker-up' are extracts from *Fame is the Spur* by Howard Spring, published by HarperCollins. Reprinted by permission of David Higham Associates.

'Handwriting' is an extract from *Further Particulars*, by C.H. Rolph, published by Oxford University Press. Reprinted by permission of David Higham Associates.

'House Ownership', 'Pocket Money' and 'The Boat Race' are extracts from *London Particulars* by C.H. Rolph, published by Oxford University Press. Reprinted by permission of David Higham Associates.

'Bolton Streetsellers' and 'Caps' are extracts from *Saintly Billy* by Bill Naughton. Reprinted by permission of Oxford University Press.

'Riches', 'Marriage of Convenience' and 'Manchester Childhood' are extracts from *Autobiography* by Sir Neville Cardus. Reprinted by permission of HarperCollins Publishers Ltd.

'Boots' and 'Educating a Soldier's Children' are extracts from *Below Stairs* by Margaret Powell. Reprinted by permission of Toby Eady Associates Ltd.

Introduction

By Richard Armitage, son of the late Edward Armitage

My father was a schoolmaster. He was a physicist but he had an eclectic interest in many areas of education, which he saw as preparation for life in the widest sense and not something which could be measured simply in terms of examination results or other academic achievements. He was born in 1910 when the world in general and daily life in particular was very different from what it is today. Indeed it is difficult to imagine that any generation has ever seen or will ever see such a degree of change in their lifetimes. My father was fascinated by the impact of change on daily life and in his retirement he began to assemble a collection of written material describing aspects of daily life as it was before the 'modern era'.

I was unaware of this project until four years ago when my father spent some time in hospital and I agreed to help him bring it to fruition. Many letters were written to track down the relevant rights holders and Peter Askem, a former colleague of my father's, kindly agreed to provide illustrations.

It was my father, however, who made the contact with Robson Books which resulted in his signing a publishing contract. He was immensely proud of that achievement and it is very sad that his final illness and recent death deprived him of the opportunity to enjoy to the full the culmination of a project on which he had worked for over ten years. This book therefore represents his legacy, a window on aspects of our history which are not widely written about but which, in view of their impact on daily life, were of most direct concern to ordinary people.

Richard Armitage
Saffron Walden
July 2001

The Way We Lived –
in the Country

The Insularity of Village Life

When holidays in China and India are not uncommon and when television daily brings us pictures of cricket matches in Australia and life in the jungles of South America, it is difficult to imagine that less than a hundred years ago, villagers in England often spent their entire lives without ever venturing more than two or three miles from their place of birth.

The insularity of village life in the first half of the nineteenth century is difficult for us to imagine. While drovers trod the old green ways of England, driving flocks and herds on foot to distant markets, and while soldiers, voluntarily or conscripted, departed to fight battles in alien lands, most villagers lived out their lives within the parish boundaries.

It was in 1826 that Cobbett, lost in the lanes along the Wiltshire/Hampshire border north of Andover, encountered a woman in a cottage garden near Tangley. She was, he judged, about thirty and had two children with her. He asked her the way to Ludgershall, which was not more than four miles away, and she didn't know. She had never been there, nor to Andover (six miles away), nor to Marlborough (nine miles away). The limits of her travels, from the cottage in which she was born, had been 'up in the parish and over to Chute'. About 2½ miles.

Cobbett was most impressed and rounded off his account of the episode with a few further examples from his experience. The author cannot resist adding one of his own. Visiting the Isle of Man in the early 1950s, he met a lady whose mother had lived all her life on the island without ever once seeing the sea! There is only one parish in the Isle of Man that lacks a section of sea coast, and that is where she spent her life. She never even went down to the town of Douglas.

It will be noted that these two anecdotes concern women. Men were more likely to be called upon to make a journey or two, in the course of work or business, at some time during their lives. A woman's place was in the home. There was no reason for her to step far outside it. Even in the more enlightened days towards the end of the century, village housewives in Pitton and Farley customarily visited Salisbury, their market town, only twice a year. Once at Easter, to renew their wardrobe, and in autumn, for Salisbury Fair, held about 18 October. Even so, pious mothers tended to forgo the pleasures of the fair, as an example to their growing daughters, whom they tried to shelter from the temptations of the wicked city! And as for clothes, the village carrier was used to taking notes to the city drapers and bringing home, on sale or return, parcels of even the most intimate feminine garments. So there was really no need for a conscientious housewife to go to town at all.

A Victorian Village by Ralph Whitlock

The Family Pig

The family pig contributed greatly to a country family's sustenance in 1880.

The family pig was everybody's pride and everybody's business. Mother spent hours boiling up the 'little taturs' to mash and mix with the pot-liquor, in which food had been cooked, to feed to the pig for its evening meal and help out the expensive barley meal. The children, on their way home from school, would fill their arms with sow thistle, dandelion, and choice long grass, or roam along the hedgerows on wet evenings collecting snails in a pail for the pig's supper. These piggy crunched up with great relish. 'Feyther', over and above farming out the sty, bedding down, doctoring, and so on, would even go without his nightly half-pint when, towards the end, the barley-meal bill mounted until 'it fair frightened anybody'.

Sometimes when the weekly income would not run to a sufficient quantity of fattening food, an arrangement would be made with the baker or miller that he should give credit now, and when the pig was killed receive a portion of the meat in advance. More often than not one-half of the pig-meat would be mortgaged in this way, and it was no uncommon thing to hear a woman say, 'Us be going to kill half a pig, please God, come Friday,' leaving the uninitiated to conclude that the other half would still run about in the sty.

Some of the families killed two separate half pigs a year; others one, or even two, whole ones, and the meat provided them with bacon for the winter or longer. Fresh meat was a luxury only seen in a few of the cottages on Sunday, when sixpennyworth of pieces would be bought to make a meat pudding. If a small joint came their way as a Saturday night bargain, those without oven grates would roast it by suspending it on a string before the fire, with one of the children in attendance as turnspit. Or a 'pot-roast' would be made by placing the meat with a little lard or other fat in an iron saucepan and keeping it well shaken over the fire. But, after all, as they said, there was nothing to beat a 'toad'. For this the meat was enclosed whole in a suet crust and well boiled, a method which preserved all the delicious juices of the meat and provided a good pudding into the bargain. When some superior person tried to give them a hint, the women used to say, 'You tell us how to get the victuals: we can cook it all right when we've got it'; and they could.

When the pig was fattened – and the fatter the better – the date of execution had to be decided upon. It had to take place sometime during the first two quarters of the moon: for, if the pig was killed when the moon was waning the bacon would shrink in cooking, and they wanted it to 'plimp up'. The next thing was to engage the travelling pork butcher, or pig-sticker, and, as he was a thatcher by day, he always had to kill after dark, the scene being lighted with lanterns and the fire of burning straw which at the later stage of the proceedings was to singe the bristles of the victim.

The killing was a noisy, bloody business, in the course of which the animal was hoisted to a rough bench that it might bleed thoroughly and so preserve the quality of the meat. The job was often bungled, the pig sometimes getting away and having to be chased; but country people of that day had little sympathy for the sufferings of animals, and men, women, and children would gather round to see the sight.

After the carcass had been singed, the pig-sticker would pull off the detachable, gristly, outer covering of the toes, known locally as 'the shoes', and fling them among the children, who scrambled for them, then sucked and gnawed them, straight from the filth of the sty and blackened by fire as they were.

The whole scene, with its mud and blood, flaring lights and dark shadows, was as savage as anything to be seen in an African jungle.

But hidden from the children, there was another aspect of the pig-killing. Months of hard work and self-denial were brought on that night to a successful conclusion. It was a time to rejoice, and rejoice they did, with beer flowing freely and the first delicious dish of pig's fry sizzling in the frying-pan.

The next day, when the carcass had been cut up, joints of pork were distributed to those neighbours who had sent similar ones at their own pig-killing. Small plates of fry and other oddments were sent to others as a pure compliment, and no one who happened to be ill or down on his luck at these occasions was every forgotten.

Then the housewife 'got down to it', as she said. Hams and sides of bacon were salted, to be taken out of the brine later and hung on the wall near the fireplace to dry. Lard was dried out, hog's puddings were made, and the chitterlings were cleaned and turned three days in succession under running water, according to ancient ritual. It was busy time, but a happy one, with the larder full and something over to give away, and all the pride and importance of owning such riches.

On the following Sunday came the official 'pig feast', when fathers and mothers, sisters and brothers, married children and grandchildren who lived within walking distance arrived to dinner.

Lark Rise by Flora Thompson

Houses in the Late Nineteenth Century

In an Oxfordshire village in 1880, this is how the poorer people lived:

From the hamlet the road led on the one hand to church and school, and on the other to the main road, or the turnpike, as it was still called, and so to the market town where the Saturday shopping was done. It brought little traffic past the hamlet. An occasional farm wagon, piled with sacks or square-cut bundles of hay; a farmer on horseback or in his gig; the baker's little old white-tilted van; a string of blanketed hunters with grooms, exercising in the early morning; and a carriage with gentry out paying calls in the afternoon were about the sum of it. No motors, no buses, and only one of the old penny-farthing high bicycles at rare intervals. People still rushed to their cottage doors to see on the latter come past.

A few of the houses had thatched roofs, whitewashed outer walls and diamond-paned windows, but the majority were just stone or brick boxes with blue-slated roofs. The older houses were relics of pre-enclosure days and were still occupied by descendants of the original squatters, themselves at that time elderly people. One old couple owned a donkey and cart, which they used to carry their vegetables, eggs, and honey to the market town and sometimes hired out at sixpence a day to their neighbours. One house was occupied by a retired farm bailiff, who was reported to have 'well feathered his own nest' during his years of stewardship. Another aged man owned and worked upon about an acre of land. These, the innkeeper, and one other man, a stonemason who walked the three miles to and from his work in the town every day, were the only ones not employed as agricultural labourers.

Some of the cottages had two bedrooms, others only one, in which case it had to be divided by a screen or curtain to accommodate parents and children. Often the big boys of a family slept downstairs, or were put out to sleep in the second bedroom of an elderly couple whose own children were out in the world. Except at holiday times, there were no big girls to provide for, as they were all out in service. Still, it was often a tight fit, for children swarmed, eight, ten, or even more in some families, and although they were seldom all at home together, the eldest often being married before the youngest was born, beds and shakedowns were often so closely packed that the inmates had to climb over one bed to get into another.

But Lark Rise must not be thought of as a slum set down in the country. The inhabitants lived an open-air life; the cottages were kept clean by much scrubbing with soap and water, and doors and windows stood wide open when the weather permitted. When the wind cut across the flat land to the east, or came roaring down from the north, doors and windows had to be closed; but then, as the hamlet people said, they got more than enough fresh air through the keyhole.

There were two epidemics of measles during the decade, and two men had accidents in the harvest fields and were taken to hospital; but, for years together, the doctor was only seen there when one of the ancients was dying of old age, or some difficult first confinement baffled the skill of the old woman who, as she said, saw the beginning and end of everybody. There was no cripple or mental defective in the hamlet, and except for a few months when a poor woman was dying of cancer, no invalid. Though food was rough and teeth were neglected, indigestion was unknown, while nervous troubles, there as elsewhere, had yet to be invented. The very word 'nerve' was used in a different sense to the modern one. 'My word! An' 'aven't she got a nerve!' they would say of any one who expected more than was reasonable.

In nearly all the cottages there was but one room downstairs, and many of these were poor and bare, with only a table and a few chairs and stools for furniture and a superannuated potato-sack thrown down by way of hearthrug. Other rooms were bright and cosy, with dressers of crockery, cushioned chairs, pictures on the walls and brightly coloured hand-made rag rugs on the floor. In these there would be pots of geraniums, fuchsias, and old-fashioned sweet-smelling musk on the window-sills. In the other cottages there were grandfathers' clocks, gate-legged tables, and rows of pewter, relics of a time when life was easier for country folk.

The interiors varied, according to the number of mouths to be fed and the thrift and skill of the housewife, or the lack of those qualities; but the income in all was precisely the same, for ten shillings a week was the standard wage for the farm labourer at that time in that district.

The only sanitary arrangement known in the hamlet was housed either in a little beehive-shaped building at the bottom of the garden or in a corner of the wood and toolshed known as 'the hovel'. It was not even an earth closet; but merely a deep pit with a seat set over it, the half-yearly emptying of which caused every door and window in the vicinity to be sealed. Unfortunately, there was no means of sealing the chimneys!

The privies' were as good an index as any to the characters of their owners. Some were horrible holes; others were fairly decent, while some, and these not a few, were kept well cleared, with the seat scrubbed to snow-whiteness and the brick floor raddled. One old woman even went so far as to nail up a text as a finishing touch. 'Thou God seest me' – most embarrassing to a Victorian child who had been taught that no one must even see her approach the door.

In other words such places health and sanitary maxims were scrawled with lead pencil or yellow chalk on the whitewashed walls. Most of them embodied sound sense and some were expressed in sound verse, but few were so worded as to be printable. On short and pithy maxim may pass: 'Eat well, work well, sleep well, and – well once a day.'

Lark Rise by Flora Thompson

Transporting Timber
in the 1880s

Conveyance of tree trunks along country roads before the age of the horse gave way to motorised transport.

A load of oak timber was to be sent away before dawn at morning to a building whose works were in a town many miles off. The trunks were chained down to a heavy timber carriage with enormous red wheels, and four of the most powerful of Melbury's horses were harnessed in front to draw them.

The horses wore their bells that day. There were sixteen to the team, carried on a frame above each animal's shoulders, and turned to scale, so as to form two octaves, running from the highest note on the right or offside of the leader to the lowest on the left or nearside of the shaft-horse. Melbury was among the last to retain horse-bells in that neighbourhood; for living at Little Hintock, where the lanes yet remained as narrow as before the days of turnpike roads, these sound-signals were still as useful to him and his neighbours as they had every been in former times. Much backing was saved in the course of a year by the warning notes they cast ahead; moreóver, the tones of all the teams in the district being known to the carters of each, they could tell a long way off on a dark night whether they were about to encounter friends or strangers.

The load being a ponderous one, the lane crooked, and the air so thick, Winterborne set out, as he often did, to accompany the team as far as the corner, where it would turn into a wider road.

So they rumbled on, shaking the foundations of the roadside cottages by the weight of their progress, the sixteen bells chiming harmoniously over all.

Then occurred one of the very incidents against which the bells were an endeavour to guard. Suddenly there beamed into their eyes, quite close to them, the two lamps of a carriage, haloed by the fog. Its approach had been quite unheard by reason of their own noise. The carriage was a covered one, while behind it could be discerned another vehicle laden with luggage.

Winterborne went to the head of the team, and heard the coachman telling the carter that he must turn back. The carter declared that this was impossible.

'You can turn if you unhitch your string-horses,' said the coachman.

'It is much easier for you to turn than for us,' said Winterborne. 'We've five ton of timber on these wheels if we've an ounce.'

'But I've another carriage with luggage at my back.'

Winterborne admitted the strength of the argument. 'But even with that,' he said, 'you can back better than we. And you ought to, for you could hear our bells half a mile off.'

'And you could see our lights.'

'We couldn't, because of the fog.'

'Well, our time's precious,' said the coachman haughtily. 'You are only going to some trumpery little village or other in the neighbourhood, while we are going straight to Italy.'

'Driving all the way, I suppose?' said Winterborne sarcastically.

The contention continued in these terms till a voice from the interior of the carriage inquired what was the matter. It was a lady's.

She was informed of the timber people's obstinacy; and then Giles could hear her telling the footman to direct the timber people to turn their horses' heads.

The message was brought, and Winterborne sent the bearer back to say that he begged the lady's pardon, but that he could not do as she requested; that though he would not assert it to be impossible, it was impossible by comparison with the slight difficulty to her party to back their light carriages. As fate would have it, the incident with Grace Melbury on the previous day made Giles less gentle than he might otherwise have shown himself, his confidence in the sex being rudely shaken.

In fine, nothing could move him, and the carriages were compelled to back till they reached one of the sidings or turnouts constructed in the bank for the purpose. Then the team came on ponderously, and the clanging of its sixteen bells as it passed the discomfited carriages tilted up against the bank, lent a particularly triumphant tone to the team's progress – a tone which, in point of fact, did not at all attach to it conductor's feelings.

Giles walked behind the timber; and just as he had got past the yet stationary carriages he heard a lofty voice say, 'Who is that rude man?'

The Woodlanders by Thomas Hardy

Earth Closets

The village is Tregonissey, which the author describes as 'a very ordinary little old Cornish hamlet'. The time is 1910.

It was a good thing the village was in a healthy situation for man had done nothing to make it hygienic. I doubt if there was a single water-closet in the whole place. Most houses shared earth-closets, one to two or three houses; you can imagine to what quarrels that led with regard respective rights and duties. However, the lives of the simple must be filled with something, and their innumerable quarrels and incessant bickerings helped to fill the gap. Some houses had no closets at all. Ours was situated at the very top of the gardens at the back of the house, half-way up the hillside: hardly conducive to that good regulation of the bowels upon which the French are so candidly, and so volubly, insistent. Nobody, I think, had water inside the house: the villagers fetched all their water from the two public taps, which were, along with our shop, the chief news-centres and meeting-places the village afforded. We were the nearest to the unwonted luxury of having water within the house, for we had a tap of our own at the door – and a very capricious and skittish instrument it was to those who did not know its ways: it sent up a ferocious squirt of water in the face of the inexpert. Small children who could not resist its appeal were always getting into trouble with it, drenching themselves and their elders. For years I was afraid of it.

Sometimes water failed altogether and we took our pitchers to the clear-running stream which came out of the springs in the hillside and ran along in front of the houses at the other end of the village. That stream was a constant resource to us children: walking in the water was a fearful pleasure, all the more exquisite because we knew the penalties it would entail on arriving home; then there was damming it up with mud and floating sticks down its course, once even trying to track its lower reaches down through the fields below the village as far as Donkey Lane – that adventure gave me at least the sensation of an earlier discoverer of America. Very rarely even this stream gave out and we were forced, with carts and barrels and buckets and pails, to go all the way to Phernyssick, half a mile uphill for water. It was almost worth the journey; for in that deep cranny in the earth, a little dell overshadowed by elder-trees, there was the most delicious, the purest and coldest water you ever drank. Perhaps because, too, of the effort of getting there, we sat down and drank cup after cup of icy water as if it were pure nectar. Years later, when an undergraduate undergoing an operation in hospital, hot with fever and thirst, I remember asking my father to bring me a bottle of water from Phernyssick as the thing above all I wanted. He brought me a bottle from the deepest depths of the clay pit where he was working, a pure cold stream: it did not disappoint. When we sang the psalm in church, 'By the waters of Babylon we sat down and wept', it was always the waters of Phernyssick that I saw myself sitting by, and upon the elder-trees there that I hanged up my harp.

A Cornish Childhood by A.L. Rowse

The Village Festival

Festivals in remote villages in the early years of the twentieth century were important.

There were two great days in the village year. One was the Feast Day, which occurred on the first Sunday after 19 July. On the following Tuesday there were village sports, for which everybody had a half day off. In my childhood we looked forward to this time because a small fair came to the village. It consisted of a little roundabout and a stall at which gaudy objects were sold. In the sports the children would run races for sixpences, which would quickly be spent at the fair.

This very special holiday is maintained in our village to this day and in most of the villages of the district, although the old type of fair has disappeared. It is a time of reunion for the villagers. Friends and relations come from far and near to spend the day together. I still attend these gatherings.

The other important day – not now observed – was called Leaving Day. It mainly concerned the single men in service on the farm and the domestic girl workers. In a way there were two 'leaving days'. The married families always moved to a job on 6 April, and not on any other day. The young people's Leaving Day was 15 May. On that May morning all the married would have been installed, and were prepared to take charge for the week while the young people would be away.

The living-in servants of both sexes drew their money in golden sovereigns on 15 May. They then trooped down to the village to pay the year's accounts with the tailor and the shoemaker. It was customary to have one pair of new hand-made boots every three years, costing 30s. Suits, which were brought less frequently, were priced at from £2 to £3. On settling day the tailor and the shoemaker always provided a dish of stuffed chine for their customers.

The Monday after 15 May was a big day for these young people. It was the May Fair in the town of Sleaford. While they enjoyed the fun of the fair, they had the thrill of being hired by a new employer if they were not 'staying on'. In the streets there was only one question: 'Have you got a place?'

The wages paid in my boyhood amounted to £3 a year on leaving school for girls, and £5 for boys. The second year, £5 and £8 respectively. The third year the sum was £16 for boys, who in that third year were known as 'seconds' – that, is, second to the wagoner. After that they were usually full-blown wagoners, rising from £20 to £26 on a twelve-horse farm and upwards. Girls earned up to £20 a year. When my mother started work at the age of twelve, she received 10s from Christmas to May, with the material for a print frock, and the next year 30s for the full year, with material for an afternoon dress.

Bright Boots by Fred Gresswell

The Fire

Time was when all household life in rural communities, from the oldest to the youngest, revolved round an open fire which was never allowed to die out.

The entire household revolved around the fire, which provided warmth, cooking facilities and a social centre around which we gathered at night to chat or to read. My father had his own particular chair to the right of the fire beside the bellows and it was his job to turn the wheel to keep the fire glowing. Behind the bellows a cricket often chirped, making its own contribution to our conversations. To my father's left and under the oil lamp sat my mother, usually darning or patching, for it was a continual struggle to keep six pairs of childish heels, knees and elbows from breaking out. To the left of the fire stretched a long timber stool or form on which we children sat in a row, feet swinging above the floor. The chair next to our form belonged to our nearest neighbour and daily visitor, Bill, and other chairs in the circle were occupied by older members of the family or other visiting neighbours. If the circle of people became too big and we ran out of chairs, another timber form, which seated three or four depending on their circumference, was brought into service from inside the kitchen table.

Family hygiene also depended on the fire because every Saturday night the big twenty-gallon pot of boiling water bubbled over it and the washing commenced of an assortment of little bodies which were encased in the mud, grass, earth, hay dust and chaff that perfumed our daily lives like our own country version of *eau de cologne*. Our hair was fine-combed to evict the tenants of our time, for if this was not done on a regular basis then they established squatters' rights and proved highly undesirable lodgers. On Monday morning the big pot again came into action for the weekly wash-day, which took a full day's hard labour because keeping clean was no easy job in the country.

From the kitchen fire came the 'seeds' to light the other fires in the house. A big, battered farmyard shovel, minus the handle, was filled with blazing *gríosach* and carried, a whirl of smoke behind it, at a lively pace into the parlour. It was also used to carry the seeds to upstairs bedrooms and later I would lie in bed listening to the fire crackling and watching the figures of light and shade dancing up the walls and across the low ceiling.

The kitchen fire stood at the centre of our lives, an eternal flame never to be quenched. Only when houses were finally abandoned were their kitchen fires allowed to die out, and when one of our neighbours built a new house he carried the seed of the fire across the haggard in a bucket from the old house to the new. The fire was the heart of every home and its warm glow was never extinguished while people still lived in the house.

To School through the Fields by Alice Taylor

Sunday Chapel

A villager muses on the many Sunday services he attended in his early childhood at the turn of the century.

My parents were big chapel people. We had no pictures in the house, but we had texts. To one at the head of my bed said: 'Be sure your sins will find you out.' The one at the foot of the bed said: 'My Grace is sufficient for thee.' Those whom my mother called 'the bettermos' sort of people' went to church. Our sort of people went to chapel.

In the three villages in our district which neighboured the halls of landed gentry there were churches but no chapels. Digby, however, had a manor house, not a hall, which made us rather superior to the poorer villages, and therefore we had a Wesleyan chapel as well as a church. Villages with neither Hall nor Manor house were considered lower still in the social scale and had only a Primitive Methodist or even a Reform church.

In those days 90 per cent of the population went somewhere to worship, and we children certainly had our fair share of religious instruction. In the first place we attended a church school, where we started every day with a scripture lesson, learning catechisms, psalms and hymns parrot-fashion. This, however, was an everyday affair and had no effect on the emotions. Sundays at chapel were different.

There we started the day with Sunday-school in the mornings. The main theme was the after-life, and the prospects of going to Heaven if you were good and to Hell if you were not. There was a fire-and-brimstone flavour about the teaching on the one hand, and, on the other, the picture of even Heaven itself was not attractive to children who were having a healthy and enjoyable time on earth.

Death seemed to permeate all forms of worship, particularly the hymns, and even the pleasant ones were about angels above the bright blue sky.

We also attended two chapel services later in the day. For children these were boring at best. The sermons meant little to us, and what they did mean was neither happy nor pleasant. Our preoccupation was to watch the big clock in the centre of the chapel. At the evening service I used to let my mind dwell pleasantly on what would be happening in a quarter of an hour after we had left chapel, when we should be sitting down to cold ham and hot vegetables, which had been put in the oven to warm up before we left home. Occasionally we stayed on for the prayers meeting after the evening service. This gave the members of the congregation an opportunity to express their religious emotions in a public way.

It was normally led by a man with a ready flow of evangelist fervour, followed by the less articulate brethren, whose halting sentences were intermingled with shouts of 'Praise the Lord!' and 'Hallelujah!'

Bright Boots by Fred Gresswell

The Workhouse

The shame of the dreaded workhouse had its effect on the lives and fears of the aged in Victorian England and even into the early decades of the twentieth century.

If you survived melancholia and rotting lungs it was possible to live long in this valley. Joseph and Hannah Brown, for instance, appeared to be indestructible. For as long as I could remember they had lived together in the same house by the common. They had lived there, it was said, for fifty years; which seemed to me for ever. They had raised a large family and sent them into the world, and had continued to live on alone, with nothing left of their noisy brood save some dog-eared letters and photographs.

The old couple were as absorbed in themselves as lovers, content and self-contained; they never left the village or each other's company, they lived as snug as two podded chestnuts. By day blue smoke curled up from their chimney, at night the red windows glowed; the cottage, when we passed it, said 'Here live the Browns', as though that were part of nature.

Though white and withered, they were active enough, but they ordered their lives without haste. The old woman cooked, and threw grain to the chickens, and hung out her washing on bushes; the old man fetched wood and chopped it with a billhook, did a bit of gardening now and then, or just sat on a seat outside his door and gazed at the valley, or slept. When summer came they bottled fruit, and when winter came they ate it. They did nothing more than was necessary to live, but did it fondly, with skill – then sat together in their clock-ticking kitchen enjoying their half-century of silence. Whoever called to see them was welcomed gravely, be it man or beast or child; and to me they resembled two tawny insects, slow but deft in their movements; a little foraging, some frugal feeding, then any amount of stillness. They spoke to each other without raised voices, in short chirrups as brief as bird-song, and when they moved about in their tiny kitchen they did so smoothly and blind, gliding on worn, familiar rails, never bumping or obstructing each other. They were fond, pink-faced, and alike as cherries, having taken and merged, through their years together, each other's looks and accents.

It seemed that the old Browns belonged for ever, and that the miracle of their survival was made commonplace by the durability of their love – if one should call it love, such a balance. Then suddenly, within the space of two days, feebleness took them both. It was as though two machines, wound up and synchronized, had run down at exactly the same time. Their interdependence was so legendary we didn't notice their plight at first. But after a week, not having been seen about, some neighbours thought it best to call. They found old Hannah on the kitchen floor feeding her man with a spoon. He was lying in a corner half-covered with matting, and they were both too weak to stand. She had chopped up a plate of peelings, she said, as she hadn't been able to manage the fire. But they were all right really, just a touch of the damp; they'd do, and it didn't matter.

Well, the Authorities were told; the Visiting Spinsters got busy; and it was decided they would have to be moved. They were too frail to help each other now, and their children were too scattered, too busy. There was but one thing to be done; it was for the best; they would have to be moved to the Workhouse.

The old couple were shocked and terrified, and lay clutching each other's hands. 'The Workhouse' – always a word of shame, grey shadow falling on the close of life, most feared by the old (even when called The Infirmary); abhorred more than debt, or prison, or beggary, or even the stain of madness.

Hannah and Joseph thanked the visiting Spinsters but pleaded to be left at home, to be left as they wanted, to cause no trouble, just simply to stay together. The Workhouse could not give them the mercy they needed, but could only divide them in charity. Much better to hide, or die in a ditch, or to starve in one's familiar kitchen, watched by the objects one's life had gathered – the scrubbed empty table, the plates and saucepans, the cold grate, the white stopped clock . . .

'You'll be well looked after,' the Spinsters said, 'and you'll see each other twice a week.' The bright busy voices cajoled with authority and the old couple were not trained to defy them. So that same afternoon, white and speechless, they were taken away to the Workhouse. Hannah Brown was put to bed in the Women's Wing, and Joseph lay in the Men's. It was the first time, in all their fifty years, that they had ever been separated. They did not see each other again, for in a week they were both dead.

I was haunted by their end as by no other, and by the kind, killing Authority that arranged it. Divided, their life went out of them, so they ceased as by mutual agreement. Their cottage stood empty on the edge of the common, its front door locked and soundless. Its stones grew rapidly cold and repellent with its life so suddenly withdrawn. In a year it fell down, first the roof, then the walls, and lay scattered in a tangle of briars. Its decay was so violent and overwhelming, it was as though the old couple had wrecked it themselves.

Soon all that remained of Joe and Hannah Brown, and their long close life together, were some grass-grown stumps, a garden gone wild, some rusty pots, and a dog-rose.

Cider with Rosie by Laurie Lee

Health

A mixture of hard work, good food and simple hygiene laid the foundations for the good health of a Leicestershire farmer's son in the 1920s.

Whether due to the right mixture of work, food, hygiene and sleep, or to my sturdy yeoman ancestors, my childhood was healthy. It was axiomatic in the family that you looked after what you had, and that included a Puritanic regard for fitness. We boys followed certain guidelines laid down by Mother to combat bad weather. When doing a necessary outdoor task, it mattered not how wet you became. Feet might be sodden and rain running down your neck, but no harm would befall you if you kept working. If you didn't, 'You'd catch something you wouldn't easily get rid of.' So out in the fields in wet weather, fencing, muck knocking, spudding thistles or foddering, we ate our lunch sandwiches with scarcely a break. Consumption, the scourge of adolescents in my youth, was the disease Mother feared most. We were reminded of every local person who had died of 'chest trouble' in living memory – Mother's, that is. Though I never knew him, I had a vivid picture of how old Taylor ended: how he got so wet and cold sleeping in a ditch at lunchtime that he collapsed and died. When they found him his limbs were so stiff and distorted they buried him in a shroud because he would fit no coffin. I knew of every last moment of old Hackney who died of double pneumonia because he sold his jacket to pay for beer and insisted he could keep warm enough if he stuffed hay between his shirt and his skin. But most horrendous to my imagination was the fate of the schoolboy who went on a Sunday school 'treat' to Matlock, became hot through climbing and sat in a cave to cool off. 'Dead within a fortnight,' was Mother's verdict. Hence, when arriving home wet from the fields it was an article of faith to bath in the back kitchen and don dry clothes before eating a meal.

More specifically relevant to good teeth, we drank plenty of milk. Milk puddings or custard accompanied all other puddings, while bread and milk with added sugar was frequently our supper. But we also drank milk in less orthodox fashion. No one really knows the flavour of cows' milk who has not drunk it straight from the cow. It is an art only to be attempted by the accomplished milker, and quite on a par with drinking wine remotely from a Spanish flagon. The skill lies in turning the cow's teat sideways and upwards, and squirting the milk straight into the open mouth. The taste of the warm milk as it spatters off the back teeth or the hard palate is delicious, and as different from the bottled stuff as a fresh peach from a tinned one.

It is one thing to make good teeth, another to keep them. We cleaned our teeth with water and soap, and occasionally soot if we wanted to get an extra shine. Not until well into my teens did I encounter dentifrice. But I still maintained that my greatest aid dental hygiene was the apple. Good 'eaters' were available all year round. Running the length of the house were attics in which were stored the apples from half an acre of orchard; cookers on one side, eaters on the other. Every night before getting into bed we groped our way up the unlit attic stairs, to select the variety of our fancy; 'groped' because candles were forbidden up there, and we relied on the pale light reflected from the bedroom.

A Yeoman's Son by H. St G. Cramp

Pre-Nuptial Arrangements in 1594

Elizabeth Spencer, a great heiress, makes things clear to her fiancé, Lord Compton in 1594.

My sweet life, now I have declared to you my mind for the settling of your estate, I suppose that it were best for me to bethink and consider within myself what allowance were meetest for me . . . I pray and beseech you to grant to me, your most kind and loving wife, the sum of £2600 quarterly to be paid. Also I would, besides that allowance, have £600 quarterly to be paid, for the performance of charitable works; and those things I would not, neither will be accountable for. Also, I will have three horses for my own saddle, that none shall dare to lend or borrow: none lend but I, none borrow but you.

Also, I would have two gentlewomen, lest one should be sick, or have some other-let. Also, believe it, it is an undecent thing for a gentlewoman to stand mumping alone, when God hath blessed their lord and lady with a great estate. Also, when I ride a hunting, or a hawking, or travel from one house to another, I will have them attending; so, for either of those said women, I must and will have for either of them a horse. Also, I will have six or eight gentlemen; and I will have my two coaches, one lined with velvet to myself, with four very fine horses; and a coach for my women, lined with cloth and laced with gold, or otherwise with scarlet and laced with silver, with four good horses.

Also, I will have two coachmen; one for my own coach, the other for my women. Also, at any time when I travel, I will be allowed not only caroches and spare horses, for me and my women, and I will have such carriages to be fitting for all, orderly, not pestering my things with my women's, nor theirs with either chambermaids, nor theirs with washmaids. Also, for laundresses, when I travel, I will have them sent away before with the carriages, to see all safe. And the chambermaids I will have go before, that the chamber may be ready, sweet and clean. Also, that it is undecent for me to crowd myself with my gentleman-usher in my coach, will have him to have a convenient horse to attend me, either in city or country. And I must have two footmen. And my desire is, that you defray all the charges for me. And for myself besides my yearly allowance, I would have twenty gowns of apparel; six of them excellent good ones, eight of them for the country, and six other of them very excellent good ones. Also, I would have to put in my purse £2000 and £200, and so, you to pay my debts. Also I would have £6000 to buy me jewels; and £4000 to buy me a pearl chain.

Now, seeing I have been, and am so reasonable unto you, I pray you do find my children apparel, and their schooling, and all my servants, men and women, their wages.

A Country House Companion by Mark Girouard

Country-house Entertaining

Entertaining in large country-houses in the nineteenth century was on a huge scale.

Having people to stay is made easy when there is an abundance of space and servants. Since both were to be found in country houses, guests have featured prominently in country-house life from the Middle Ages onwards. To begin with, when roads were almost non-existent, distances great, and horse or foot the only means of transport, anyone who came to a house on business or for a meal almost automatically stayed the night. This was less the case as transport improved, but on the other hand improved transport made it easier to bring invited guests across long distances for short periods. The coming of the railways marked the great breakthrough. As a result it was in nineteenth-century country-houses that the house-party entered on its apogee, especially in the form of the 'Saturday to Monday' (the expression 'weekend' was considered vulgar in Victorian and Edwardian days).

At country stations all over the British Isles trains disgorged crowds of ladies and gentlemen from first class compartments, valets and lady's maids from third class compartments, leather trunks and (in the days of the late Victorian bicycling craze) bicycles from the luggage van. All were conveyed in fleets of carriages (for the gentry) and 'brakes' (for the servants) to neighbouring country houses to spend two or three days, or sometimes two or three weeks together. House parties were not necessarily held just for pleasure. They could be a way of pushing social or political ambitions, or putting one's daughters in company with eligible young men. Their make-up was as carefully worked out as the make-up of a dinner-party, and the names of the guests were listed in the social columns of the London newspapers. To have thirty or forty house guests was nothing out of the ordinary in a big country house.

Much of our knowledge of country houses comes from the letters or diaries written by guests. To have the freedom of a big house set in several square miles of woods and parkland, to share it with congenial company, to hunt, shoot, fish, gossip, argue, sightsee, flirt or play games together, could add up to one of the pleasantest ways of passing time every devised. But the ideal was not always attained; some house parties were more an affair of rich people eating too much and being bored together in the rain.

A Country House Companion by Mark Girouard

Country-houses

An enormous amount of organisation was involved in the maintenance of the great country-house in the first half of the nineteenth century.

Here in the country-house was the accumulated tradition not only of culture but of order. The life of a great country-house afforded a microcosm of the state: no fitter training ground could have been devised for those called upon by birth and wealth to rule. An English landed estate in the first half of the nineteenth century was a masterpiece of smooth and intricate organisation with its carefully-graded hierarchy of servants, indoors and outdoor, and its machinery for satisfying most of the normal wants of communal life – farms, gardens, diaries, brewhouses, granaries, stables, laundries and workshops; carpenters, ironmongers, painters, masons, smiths and glaziers; its kitchens, larders, and sculleries, beer and wine cellars, gunrooms and stores. At Woburn the Duke of Bedford directly employed nearly 600 persons, 300 artificers being regularly paid every Saturday night, and his bill for domestic pensions alone amounted to over £2000 a year. Here, Greville reported, 'is order, economy, grandeur, comfort and general content . . . with inexhaustible resources for every taste – a capital library, all the most curious and costly books, pictures, prints, interesting portraits, gallery of sculpture, gardens, with the rarest exotics, collected and maintained at a vast expense.' Almost every county had at least one Woburn and a dozen or score of hereditary mansions on a smaller but comparable scale.

English Saga 1840-1940 by Sir Arthur Bryant

The Way We Lived –
in the Towns

London in 1660

This is London during the year of the Restoration, five years before the Great Fire.

The Restoration year of 1660 was a jolly one, for the restrictive years of Puritan rule were over. The scene on 29 May has been preserved by John Evelyn. 'This day, after a sad and long exile, and after calamitous suffering of both the king and church for seventeen years, His Majesty King Charles II came to London: this day was also his birthday. He came with a triumph of over twenty thousand horse and foot brandishing their swords and shouting with inexpressible joy. The ways were strewn with flowers, the bells were ringing, the streets were hung with tapestry, and the fountains were running wine. The mayor, aldermen and all the Companies, in their chains of gold, liveries and banners, were present; also the lords and nobles. Everybody was clad in cloth of silver, gold and velvet; the windows and balconies were all set with ladies, trumpets and music, and myriads of people flocked the streets as far as Rochester, so that they took seven hours to pass through the city – even from two in the afternoon till nine at night. I stood in the Strand and beheld it and blessed God.'

Restoration London, even after the Plague had reduced the population, was more crowded than it had ever been. Trade in all the necessities and luxuries of the world was flourishing, and along Thames Street the warehouses and cellars were bursting with commodities. But the City was not only a great mart and port; it was also a centre of considerable manufacture, as the existence of the wealthy Companies and Guilds gave evidence. The dirt came not only from refuse but also from the burning of sea-coal from Newcastle in domestic hearths as well as in the furnaces of soap-boilers, dyers, brewers and other manufacturers. Fogs were indeed as frequent in Restoration London as they were to be in Victorian London. They so distressed John Evelyn that, in his indignation, he wrote his *Fumifugium; or the Inconvenience of the Air and Smoke of London Dissipated*. It is this horrid smoke, Evelyn wrote, 'which obscures our churches and makes our palaces look old, which fouls our clothes and corrupts the waters, so that the very rain and refreshing dews which fall in the several seasons precipitate this impure vapour, which with its black and tenacious quality spots and contaminates whatever is exposed to it.' London's impure mists and filthy vapours, Evelyn pointed out, caused among the inhabitants of this one city more than in the whole earth besides the raging 'of vile catarrhs, phthisics, coughs and consumptions'. Yet the authorities did not discourage the burning of coal because large taxes could be raised from its import into London. The king, however, warmly commended Evelyn's proposals to mitigate the nuisance and commanded him to prepare a Bill on the matter for presentation to parliament. Five years later the whole City went up in horrid smoke.

The use of brick in the City had been encouraged for a long time, partly to reduce the number of fires but partly also to save timber which was in short supply owing to over-felling and was badly needed for building ships. Although London had had its Building Acts since those promulgated by its first Lord Mayor in 1189 whereby party walls were to be of stone or brick to stop fire spreading, they were rarely observed. Foundations might be of brick or stone, but walls of timber, lath and plaster. On street fonts the upper storeys often projected in order to give weather protection below, sometimes so much so that the inhabitants could lean out and shake hands from opposite windows. Many alleys, therefore, were often dark even in daytime.

Streets and market places were paved with cobblestones set in gravel down the middle of which ran gutters where waste water and refuse were thrown, refuse being collected from time to time by scavengers for deposit in one of the many laystalls on the outskirts of the City or along the river front. No raised pavements protected the pedestrian from passing traffic and few bollasters existed. Rain dripped straight from the eaves into the streets, for gutters and down-pipes were rare, a fact lamented by Evelyn as 'the troublesome and malicious disposal of the spouts and gutters overhead', which rendered the labyrinth of passages 'a continual wet day after the storm is over'. Sewage went either into streams like the Fleet or into cesspits below the houses, and no public lavatories existed: even Mrs Pepys had on one recorded occasion to stoop in public and 'there in a corner do her business'

Wren's London by Eric de Mare

The Great Fire

In spite of the terror, the upheaval and dispossession caused by the Great Fire of London in 1665, it proved in the end to be a great mercy.

The wealthier merchants lived around Throgmorton Street, the Royal Exchange and Tower Street, with their counting houses at street level, apartments above and perhaps warehouses behind. Lesser breeds like shopkeepers traded from the ground floor of their homes, and there craftsmen had their workshops with living accommodation above for families and apprentices. In the wider streets the stalls and baskets of hawkers clustered thickly, while barrows, carriages, carts and sedan chairs added to the din and confusion. The dead were packed into the churchyards and the poor in great numbers into dark, squalid tenements, entire families being crammed into single rooms, often in cellars. The overcrowding was as appalling as it was to become when London exploded in Victorian times.

The medieval thoroughfares of the old City had been built to take pedestrians and pack-horses only; during the seventeenth century the considerable growth of the wheeled traffic so essential to the City's life made them totally inadequate. Year by year the traffic jams grew worse and pedestrians were driven to the walls.

Some three thousand watermen rowing for hire on the river were growing ever more anxious about their livelihoods with the increase of the Hackney Hell Carts and the new sedan chairs that had arrived in London in 1634. John Taylor, the Water Poet who became royal waterman and was the self-appointed Public Relations Officer of his kind, called attention to the plight of his fellows in a 'rattling, rowling and rumbling age'. He broke into a song of protest:

Carroaches, coaches, jades and Flanders mares
Do rob us of our shares, our wares, our fares;
Against the ground we stand and knock our heels
Whilst all our profit runs away on wheels.

In fact the wheeled traffic did not greatly affect the watermen for citizens continued to use their river as a main, wide, airy high street which provided the most pleasant, safe and rapid means of conveyance from one side of the City to the other. With the increase of population and business, wherries as well as carriages were in demand. The river also supplied a good deal of domestic water with the help of the pumping wheels, worked by the tides, that the Dutchman, Pieter Morice, had installed beneath the northern arch of the Bridge in 1580. Water supplies were, if not too clean, at least adequate as a result not only of the Bridge wheels but also of various springs and wells and of the channel of the New River Company.

One aggravation of the street congestion was the placing of water conduits at street crossings. Another was the blockage caused by the street markets. A third, and major one, was that of purprestures – the foolish official permits to extend buildings into the streets. Charles II tried to reduce the most serious bottlenecks by an Act of 1662, but nothing was really accomplished until the Fire ruthlessly enforced a solution to the whole problem of street improvement.

The City, in fact, provided the perfect seed bed both for plague and conflagration. Pestilence, endemic since the early Middle Ages, in some years became pandemic, and in Tudor days if deaths from plague exceeded fifty a week, all the theatres were closed to prevent its spread. Between 1094 and the Great Plague of 1665 London suffered twelve serious outbreaks. Dysentery, typhus, smallpox and the sweating sickness or *Sudor Anglicus* (mortal in three hours) were always prevalent, but the mass killer was Bubonic Plague, in 1603, in London, some thirty thousand died from it, and even more in 1625; there was a further minor outbreak in 1636 and then came the Great Plague, a return of the Black Death which had ravaged Europe three centuries before.

Bubonic Plague was carried by rats brought to London in ships; fleas sucked their blood and deposited the microbes in the bodies of human beings. Floor rushes, wall hangings, and dirty clothes and bedding harboured the fleas while the rats found comfortable quarters everywhere in the hollow walls of the houses. The outbreak began early in the summer of 1665 in the suburb of St Giles's-in-the-Fields, and soon the death roll was mounting rapidly until, as a contemporary records, 'there is a dismal solitude in London streets. Now shops are shut in, people rare, and very few that walk about, insomuch as the grass begins to spring up in some places and a deep silence in every place, especially within the walls . . . The nights are too short to bury the dead; the long summer days are spent from morning until twilight in conveying the vast number of dead bodies into the bed in their graves.'

Pepys had bravely stayed in London to carry on his navy job, and as late as 20 September he wrote: 'But Lord, what a sad time it is, to see no boats upon the river – and grass grow up and down Whitehall-court – and nobody but poor wretches in the streets.'

As well as providing comfortable quarters for rats, the hollow walls of the houses also, like chimneys, encouraged flames with rising draughts, and it was only after the Fire, when brick and stone replaced timber, when floors were boarded, tiled or carpeted, and when the brown rats (which carried fewer fleas than the black ones) began killing their darker peers with that racial discrimination of which Nature is brutally fond, that the main causes of plague and fire were at last eliminated. So, in spite of the upheaval and dispossession it imposed, the Great Fire proved in the end to be a great mercy.

Wren's London by Eric de Mare

The Industrial Revolution

The effects of the Industrial Revolution in 1800 when England had been at war for thirty-three out of the previous sixty-three years were devastating.

While Bumble and his wife still governed by ancients lights in the village, the winding road to the smoky towns in the northern dales was open to every man of enterprise. Activity followed opportunity, and wealth and power activity. The whirling wheels of Brummagem and Manchester span the pattern of a new world.

The workmanship, durability, ingenuity and variety of British goods were the wonder of the age. Visitors to Sheffield saw knives with a hundred and eighty blades and scissors so small that they were hardly visible to the eye; at Leeds one could step at nightfall into clothes which at daybreak had been raw wool from the sheep's back. Every nation's fashions were carefully studied; Latins could walk their native Boulevards in their traditional costume and yet be clad from head to toe in the products of the West Riding. William Radcliffe on his return from the Manchester cotton market used to be asked by his mill hands from what remote land the week's returns had come. He and his like won and kept their customers by honest dealing; the label 'English' was a universal passport. To the hall-mark of quality – legacy of generations of the fine craftsmanship and integrity – were added the range and cheapness of the power-machines. Demand for English wares fostered the growth of machinery, and machinery, by lowering prices, multiplied sales. National necessity and the opportunity for growing rich quickly overcame a conservative people's prejudices against the snorting, roaring monsters that revolutionised their lives. At Bradford a steam engine, rejected in 1793 as a smoky nuisance, had become by 1801 the pride of that thriving town; at South Cary Parson Woodforde watched with approval a wool-carding machine with 3,000 motions operating simultaneously.

All this, taking place in the midst of a great war, had involved an immense dislocation of social life.

The results were grave. To those who troubled to visit the new towns it seemed as though the nation had sold its soul to Mammon. Under the double effect of war and the new price-cutting economics, men, women and children were subjected to influences which endangered the future morality and physique of the race. At the moment that British patriotism was being invoked as never before to defy the French, the conception of patriotism was being discarded in economic matters for the creed of a bagman. Liberty for the thrustful to grow rich was held to justify every abuse. Ancient pieties and ways of life were uprooted in a few years by the uncontrolled action of machinery and cut-throat competition. While cultured folk deplored the sufferings of French exiles, thousands of Britons were driven from their homes and traditional crafts by enclosure and unemployment and herded like slaves into the new mills without the leaders of national opinion uttering a word in protest or even apparently being aware of the fact. In Manchester and the surrounding cotton towns children, set to the looms at seven years of age, worked from five in the morning till six at night, while the population, multiplying itself every few years, was crowded into narrow, airless, sunless streets and underground cellars. Little girls of ten, naked and black with coal dust, dragged trucks on all fours down the tunnels of Northumbrian mines, and in Birmingham men went about with thumbs crushed into formless lumps by unfenced machinery. Stench and darkness, hellish din and ignorance were becoming the lot of an ever-growing proportion of the race. And this in a Christian country whose social happiness and freedom had long been the envy of the world!

Years of Victory 1802-1812 by Sir Arthur Bryant

London in 1800

The capital was crowded and chaotic, even two hundred years ago.

One saw the spirit of freedom in the London streets: the 'multitudinous moving picture' of the Strand with the crowds coming and going like a continuous riot under the flickering oil lights; the rattle of the coaches and drays; the cheerfulness of the fashionable shops with their glistening panes and smart bow-windows huddled against lowly dwellings behind whose open doors and low, ragged hutches cobblers and other humble artisans did their work; 'the mob of happy faces crowding up at the pit door of Drury Lane theatre just at the hour of five'; the traffic blocks with the gilded carriages of the aristocracy patiently taking their turn behind droves of oxen, coal-waggons and blaspheming draymen; in the floating pall of congealed smoke that, rising from the chimneys of a hundred and sixty thousand houses and furnaces, hung for more than half a year, sometimes in impenetrable fog and at other times in a glorious, sun-pierced canopy, over the domes and spires of the City and which always put the painter Haydon in mind of energy personified. In the capital of England – 'Lunnon,' as Fox called it – everyone seemed to be absorbed in his business and everyone had to look after himself. 'You stop,' wrote a dazed foreigner, 'and bump! a porter runs against you shouting "By your leave" after he has knocked you down . . . Through din and clamour and the noise of hundreds of tongues and feet you hear the bells of the church steeples, postmen's bells, the street organs, fiddlers and the tambourines of itinerant musicians and the cries of vendors of hot and cold food at the street corners. A rocket blazes up stories high amidst a yelling crowd of beggars, sailors and urchins. Someone shouts 'Stop thief!', his handkerchief is gone. Everyone runs and presses forward, some less concerned to catch the thief than to steal a watch or purse for themselves.

Before you are aware of it a young, well-dressed girl has seized your hand, 'Come my lord, come along, let us drink a glass together!' . . . All the world rushes headlong without looking, as if summoned to the bedside of the dying. That is Cheapside and Fleet Street open on a December evening.'

Yet in all this chaotic city, with its 864,000 inhabitants and its congeries of thieves' kitchens and Alsatias, there was no police force but a handful of scarlet-waistcoated Bow Street Runners and the aged watchmen of the medieval parishes. The government of the greatest city in the world was still fundamentally that of a village. The sculptures in the Abbey were so dirty that it was impossible to distinguish the figures, the tombs were mutilated and covered with names scratched by citizens in search of a half-holiday's immortality, and outside St. Paul's stood a shabby statue of Queen Anne, lacking nose and ears, with a pile of stones at her feet- target of successive generations of urchins. The seats in St. James's Park were too rickety to use, the streets fouled and blocked by herds of cattle, the air hideous with cries extolling the rival merits of flowers and vegetables, rabbits and lavender, baked fruits from charcoal braziers, bandboxes slung on poles, baskets and rat-traps, bellows and playbills and even pails of water, for large parts of the capital lacked the most elementary conveniences. It was so all over England; at Bristol the steps of the cathedral were used habitually as a public lavatory.

Years of Victory 1802-1812 by Sir Arthur Bryant

Stage Coach

In 1830, travel was by stage coach with all its privations. Twenty years later it was obsolete.

In 1830, and in most places in 1840, a man who wanted to take a journey did so on the roof of a stage coach. Tom Brown went to Rugby of all places in the old Tally-ho! To travel by the London Tantivy mail to Birmingham along the macadamised turnpike, a distance of 120 miles, took twelve hours; to Liverpool another eleven. One left London shortly before eight in the morning, changed in the course of ten minutes into the Birmingham-Liverpool Mail at the same hour in the evening, and reached one's destination, bleary-eyed and exhausted, at seven next day.

That was the very fastest travel. And what travelling it was! On a cold damp, raw December morning one waited in the dark at the posting-house for the Highflyer or Old True Blue Independent coach 'coming hup' and, when the muddied, steaming horses drew up in the courtyard, took one's 'preference' seat in the hot, suffocating, straw-strewn box. There one sat in cramped darkness for many hours of creaking, lumbering and jolting until the 'many-coated, brandy-faced, blear-eyed guard let in a whole hurricane of wind' with the glad tidings that the coach had reached another inn 'wot 'oss'd it,' where the company was allowed half an hour's grace to dine. The only alternative was to travel on the roof, in dust and glare in summer, and muffled to the nose in a frozen eternity in winter. It had its romantic side, of course, but no man would undertake such travel lightly. And what with the fare of sixpence a mile for inside accommodation, the cost of meals at the posting inns, and the tips to ostler, boots, guards, post-boy and waiter, it was beyond the means of all but a small minority.

Yet before the end of the forties the scene has completely changed. It is an urban England that is engraved on the crowded page. The stress is now on paved streets, vast Gothic town halls, the latest machinery, above all the railroad. The iron horse, with its towering, belching funnel and its long load of roaring coaches plunging through culvert and riding viaduct, had spanned the land, eliminating distance and reducing all men to a common denominator. And the iron horse did not go from village to village: it went from industrial town to town. The England of Winchester and Canterbury and Chester was a thing of the past. The England of smoking Rotherham and Hull and colonial Crewe had arrived.

English Saga 1840-1940 by Sir Arthur Bryant

London's Services

Gas lighting was still relatively new but all life's essentials were still supplied to Londoners in the time-honoured fashion.

At night the march of progress was symbolised by the lighting of the London streets. Gas lighting had come in a couple of decades back, and was now being slowly extended from the main thoroughfares into the courts and alleys of the older London that besieged them. The great gasometers rose like fortresses above the drab rows of working-class dwellings, and from dusk till dawn the flaring gas jets made a peculiar humming that was the musical background to the nocturnal activities of the Londoner. Judged by modern standards the light they gave was dim and little diffused: to our rustic forefathers it seemed a prodigious illumination. Yet four years were to elapse before the main road from Hyde Park Corner to Kensington was lit by a single lamp.

The essential services of life were still supplied to the Londoner after a country model. Donkeys carried vegetables to Covent Garden and colliers or 'Geordies' brought their 'best Wallsend' from Tyne and Wear by sail: a prolonged west wind could cause a fuel shortage in the capital. And the wintry streets were perambulated by tall-hatted coalheavers peddling their wares. Here, too, the old cries of London were still heard: in winter crossing-sweepers sat by braziers to gather toll of familiar clients for keeping their pitch clean. In her rough white cottage in Hyde Park opposite Knightsbridge, old Ann Hicks sold gilt gingerbreads and curds and whey and took her modest toll, won by half a century of prescription, of Park brushwood and hurdles to make her fire. In the new Bayswater road one could watch haymakers in the open fields to the north: a little farther on, where the gravel Oxford turnpike fell into Notting Dale, the pig-keepers who supplied the London hotels squatted in rustic confusion. In the cellars of Westminster as well as in the suburbs Londoners still kept cows: the metropolis' milk supply was mainly home-made with, so it was hinted, liberal assistance from the pump. And on any Monday morning herds of cattle were driven by drovers armed with cudgels and iron goads through the narrow streets to Smithfield: pedestrians were sometimes gored by the poor beasts. In Smithfield Tellus kept his unsavoury rustic court: a nasty, filthy, dangerous country Bastille in the heart of London and a great offence to sensitive and progressive persons. Vested interests defended it stubbornly against all assaults: *Punch* depicted a proprietary Alderman taking his wife and family for a walk there. 'Oh! how delicious,' he declares, 'the drains are this morning!'

English Saga 1840-1940 by Sir Arthur Bryant

The New Towns

In 1845, workers in the new towns of the Industrial Revolution
lived crowded together in squalid conditions.

The new England they built was housed not so much in towns as in barracks. These were groups round the new factories, on the least expensive and therefore most congested model attainable. They were erected back to back and on the cheapest available site, in many cases marshes. There was no ventilation and no drainage. The intervals between the houses which passed for streets were unpaved and often followed the line of streams serving as a conduit for excrement.

The appearance of such towns was dark and forbidding. In a terrible passage in one of his novels of the forties, Disraeli described such a town. 'Wodgate had the appearance of a vast squalid suburb. As you advanced, leaving behind you long lines of little dingy tenements, with infants lying about the road, you expected every moment to emerge into some streets, and encounter buildings bearing some correspondence, in their size and comfort, to the considerable population swarming and busied around you. Nothing of the kind. There were no public buildings of any sort; no churches, chapels, town-hall, institute, theatre; and the principal streets in the heart of the town in which were situated the coarse and grimy shops . . . were equally narrow, and if possible more dirty. At every fourth or fifth house, alleys seldom above a yard wide, and streaming with filth, opened out of the street . . . Here, during the days of business, the sound of the hammer and the file never ceased, amid gutters of abomination, and piles of foulness, and stagnant pools of filth; reservoirs of leprosy and plague, whose exhalations were sufficient to taint the atmosphere of the whole of the kingdom and fill the country with fever and pestilence.'

Reality was more terrible than art. Disraeli did not exaggerate but, out of deference to Victorian proprieties, toned down the horror of his picture. The official reports of the Royal Health of Towns Commission of 1845 were more graphic for they were more exact. In 442 dwellings examined in Preston, 2,400 people slept in 852 beds. In 84 cases four shared a bed, in 28 five, in 13 six, in 3 seven, and in 1 eight. The cellar populations of Manchester and Liverpool, nearly 18,000 in the former and more in the latter, were without any means of removing night-soil from the habitations. Even for those who lived above ground water-closets were unknown and the privies, shared in common by hundreds, were generally without doors.

In Little Ireland, Ancoats, Engels, seeking material for his great work on the proletariat of south Lancashire, described the standing pools, full of refuse, offal and sickening filth, that poisoned the atmosphere of the densely populated valley of the Medlock. Here 'a horde of ragged women and children swarm about. . . . The race that lives in these ruinous cottages behind broken windows mended with oilskin, sprung doors and rotten door-posts, or in dark wet cellars in measureless filth and stench . . . must really have reached the lowest stage of humanity . . . In each of these pens, containing at most two rooms, a garret and perhaps a cellar, on the average twenty human beings live . . . For each one hundred and twenty persons, one usually inaccessible privy is provided; and in spite of all the preachings of the physicians, in spite of the excitement into which the cholera epidemic plunged the sanitary police by reason of the condition of Little Ireland, in spite of everything, in this year of grace, 1844, it is in almost the same state as in 1831.'

English Saga 1840-1940 by Sir Arthur Bryant

Victorian Living Conditions

By 1900, England had acquired a great empire but the living conditions of the mass of its people had still not increased in proportion to the national wealth.

The close of Queen Victoria's reign marked the end of an epoch. Her life had seen a great Empire consolidated, vast national wealth built up and Britain's prestige raised to a level it had never before attained. What had been the cost? By most people it was counted in terms of the handful of casualties and the comparatively insignificant financial outlay on the campaigns which had opened up new lands and new trade routes, bringing us untold riches. Few troubled to look deeper. Few realized that the country had paid and was still paying heavily for its remarkable commercial and industrial expansion in the marked deterioration of physique and health which the appalling conditions of labour had brought about. It is no exaggeration to say that the opening of the twentieth century saw malnutrition more rife in England than it had been since the great dearths of medieval and Tudor times. Apart from a handful of social workers there were few who showed any real concern at the terrible distress in the working-class districts. The apathy and callous indifference of the general public was clearly revealed when Seebohm Rowntree published in 1900 his study of the conditions under which the poor were living in the City of York.

It is not surprising that this pioneer paid most attention to housing and sanitation. It was a time when the science of domestic hygiene was making rapid strides. A great time had been learnt of the need for pure water supply and efficient drainage. By contrast, little was known about the influence of bad diet on health. Nevertheless, Rowntree did draw attention to the inadequacy of the diet of the poor families he had studied.

Most of them lived practically entirely on bread – and it must be remembered that all of it was white bread – while many of them did not even get enough food to satisfy their hunger. In nine cases out of ten sheer poverty was the cause.

Whitehall thought it might be advisable to hold an inquiry into the matter and an Inter-Departmental Committee was appointed.

The Committee had not sat long before it was obvious that nothing that Rowntree had said was in the least exaggerated. Witness after witness described the fearful conditions under which the poor were living and working. 'Back-to-back' houses with unpaved courts receiving the contents of the 'midden-privies' and saturated with excrement and filth; half-starved children in ragged clothing with pitiable, pallid faces and deformed limbs; areas with infant mortality of nearly 250 per 1000; parents trying to rear large families on little more than bread and tea; these, and a hundred other tragic facts, were once again made public.

The Committee made a comprehensive survey of the possible causes of the poor physique and the ill-health of the labouring population of the towns. It is understandable that they tended to give greater attention to such factors as overcrowding, bad sanitation, alcoholism, factory conditions, ignorance, etc., than to what was by far the most important cause, semi-starvation due to sheer poverty.

On the Pig's Back by Bill Naughton

Suffragettes

A few years later, the suffragettes took to the streets to claim votes for women.

Each carried a muff, and concealed in each muff was a large jagged rock of flint. They walked the few miles to town.

It was three o'clock when they came to Market Street. The day was bright and cold, and the street surged with people. Ann and Pen walked from one end to the other, taking note of the men and women who had arranged to be there in support. These silently, unobtrusively. Gathered behind them, mingling with the crowds.

'This will do,' said Ann.

Pen looked at the shop, the magnificent expanse of plate-glass glittering in the cold sunlight. 'Yes,' she said. 'Now don't stop and think. Do it.'

While their resolution was hot, they stood back half-a-dozen paces, took out their flints, and hurled them into the window. The startled people looked round to see the two women surrounded now by a body-guard unfurling the familiar defiant banner: 'Votes for women!' The words fluttered on the banner, and were cried by a score of voices, almost before the last fragment of glass had tinkled to the stone.

Then broke out the familiar pandemonium. Cheers, catcalls, voices pro and con. Someone yelled: 'It's the bloody Suffragettes again!' and there was a rush at the little band which had now begun to march down the road, Ann and Pen in the van, with the banner over their heads. The Suffragettes were fair game for any one who wanted to manhandle a woman. Ann and Pen were used to free fights in the street, and that day they had a fierce one. They were struck in their faces; they were kicked and buffeted; and before the police took effective charge their blouses were hanging in ribbons and Ann was holding her skirt in position with her hands. But it was all in the day's work – all in the work of the weary years – and still there were more years to go than yet had gone! Derided and reviled, looking like a couple of drunken harlots who had been at one another's throats, their hats slanted over their eyes and their faces clawed, they tottered between the policemen to the police-station.

Fame is the Spur by Howard Spring

House Ownership

About the same time, this author's family of five had lived well, if spartanly, on thirty shillings [£1.50] a week but house ownership, even at £300, was totally beyond their reach.

Advertisement in the *West London Observer* for 18 August in 1910:

Six-roomed houses redecorated, thoroughly done, twenty shillings. Ceilings from two shillings. Walker, 35 Godolphin Road, auxiliary postman.

And here are some housing rents and values as they appear in comparable advertisements in the same newspaper:

Furnished flat, sitting room, two bedrooms, separate kitchen, piano [*sic*], plate and linen. One guinea weekly. 5 Brooklyn Road, Shepherds Bush.

Room, furnished, suit married couple, everything for use, five shillings per week. 11 Crisp Road, Hammersmith.

Six-roomed house £195, 75-year lease, near trams; bargain; only wants seeing.

Indeed houses with 99-year leases and the offer of the freehold were commonly selling at £200. A year or two later there appeared this advertisement in the same paper:

Why pay rent when you can buy one of the splendidly appointed houses on the Crabtree Estate in the Fulham Road? Each contains pretty entrance hall, two sitting rooms, three bedrooms, bathroom and scullery. Roofs boarded and tiled, bathroom tiled, electric light fittings supplied throughout, blinds fitted to all front windows. 99 years lease. Ground rent £6. Freehold can be had. Price – £300, of which only £35 need be paid down.

Yet my parents and their intimates, I remember, thought these were totally impossible prices, putting home-ownership far beyond the reach of such as they. The Crabtree Estate, it was said, was 'all too fancy', with its built-in electric light fixtures and its fitted blinds. The electric lighting in particular was all very well, bit it 'impaired one's eyesight': I remember the phrase so well, for it set me to wondering what other kind of sight there was. The Crabtree Estate must, we thought, have been getting a huge subvention from the electric-lighting companies, upstarts who were bent on doing us out of our beloved gaslight at all costs. Our landlord never succumbed: we never had electric light until we lived in the City.

I don't know what was the 'average' artisan's wage at that time, and I have always doubted official versions, but in my mother's cookery book, dated 1910, the recipes are all based on a family income of thirty shillings a week – of which one quarter was reserved for rent. I know that the rent we paid to Mr Hamm was sixteen shillings a week, and that he got it every Friday morning with the regularity of sunrise. There were one or two houses in Gowan Avenue which had hot-water systems of some kind, but we had none. Nor was there any gas-burner in any bedroom or the bathroom. In the winter, going to bed and getting up were done in the dark, washing and bathing were done by candlelight. A bucket of hot water was carried upstairs on bath-nights, and the dilution of that with cold tap-water in the bath was a matter of sober foresight and judgement. I can't remember that any of this was regarded as in any conceivable sense a hardship.

London Particulars by C.H. Rolph

Bolton Streetsellers

The cries of the itinerant street-sellers were still to be heard in Bolton in the 1920s and 1930s.

I would often roam about the neighbourhood – I was interested in everything and everybody I saw – and size up this, that, and the other one, and consider their chances of getting to heaven. There were, for instance, the various rag-and-bone men, wheeling their handcarts along the narrow back streets, proclaiming their calling with loud unearthly wails: 'Ee, ragabone . . . donkey stone, yellow stone an' rubbin' stone, ee, ragabone . . .!' Some of them employed a form of plain-song for greater effect, leading off with a distinct labionasal note on the opening. 'Ee' – the sound intensified by the two huge and horny hands employed as a megaphone round the mouth – and the bizarre ululation would issue forth from between the lines of privy closets (there was one woman totter who could be heard miles away on Rivington Pike – or so they reckoned), to be followed by a nimble articulation of 'donkey stone, rubbin' stone an' yellow stone!' This latter part was often pitched to create an antiphonal effect, as though there were two callers, one giving the response to the other – which mournful appeal would take on the intonation of a Gregorian chant, bestirring housewives, who would scutter forth bearing armfuls of old pit clothes, worn-out skirts, and the like, with the odd one humping a burst mattress or broken bedstead. There was one certain ragman, so eloquent of voice and at times producing such rich floating tones, that one would imagine a fragment of High Mass had escaped into the backstreets. Mother would grab some old clothes and thrust them at me the moment she heard him, but somehow I almost never caught up with this fugitive character. It seemed that once he had made his final invocation he would be off, and either he was stone deaf or just came out for the chant itself, for no matter how loud I and some of the neighbours called out after him he would not stop, but would hurriedly disappear round the top of the backstreet with his rag cart.

'Poor chap,' some woman would say, 'he musta run out of rubbin' stones.'

In the front streets I'd be watching the hawkers with their pony carts, and these men went in for an honest bawling, 'Finest King Edward's – five poun' for thri'pence: – who's for King Edward's whilst they last?' There was also the washing-liquor man, with a homemade box-trolley which he trundled along the sideset, and at the same time let out his shrill cry: 'Washin' liquor, ladies! finest washin' liquor – who wants washin' liquor?' There was the black-pea seller, with an old baby-carriage in which he kept a huge pan hot; it gave off a rich enticing aroma on the cool evening air when he removed the lid to ladle out a penn'orth and he used to yell: 'Peas all 'ot – peas all 'ot! – bring your money an' you'll get a good lot!'

The crumpet man also came early evening, with his bell and husky murmur, basket balanced on his head: 'Crumpets! – now, ladies, who says for a nice fresh crumpet? Muffins – who says for a good fresh muffin? Anybody fancy an oatcake – five for tuppance!' There were many more: Sabini's, with the lively pony in the ice-cream cart, came all through the summer, and there was a knife-sharpener, also the organ-grinder, numerous street singers and others.

Saintly Billy by Bill Naughton

How We Managed

Domestic Economies

Domestic economies were practised by the ladies of Cranford in 1850. Cranford was based on a real place – Knutsford in Cheshire – in which the authoress spent much of her young life.

My next visit to Cranford was in the summer. There had been neither births, deaths, nor marriages since I was there last. Everybody lived in the same house, and wore pretty nearly the same well-preserved, old-fashioned clothes. The greatest event was, that the Miss Jenkynses had purchased a new carpet for the drawing-room. Oh the busy work Miss Matty and I had in chasing the sunbeams, as they fell in an afternoon right down on this carpet through the blindless window! We spread the newspapers over the places, and sat down to our book or our work; and, lo! in a quarter of an hour the sun had moved, and was blazing away on a fresh spot; and down again we went on our knees to alter the position of the newspapers. We were very busy, too, one whole morning, before Miss Jenkyns gave her party, in following her directions, and in cutting out and stitching together pieces of newspaper, so as to form little paths to every chair, set for the expected visitors, lest their shoes might dirty or defile the purity of the carpet. Do you make paper paths for every guest to walk upon in London?

I had often occasion to notice the use that was made of fragments and small opportunities in Cranford; the rose-leaves that were gathered ere they fell, to make into a pot-pourri for some one who had no garden; the little bundles of lavender-flowers sent to strew the drawers of some town-dweller, or to burn in the chamber of some invalid. Things that many would despise, and actions which it seemed scarcely worth while to perform, were all attended to in Cranford. Miss Jenkyns stuck an apple full of cloves, to be heated and smell pleasantly in Miss Brown's room; and as she put in each clove, she uttered a Johnsonian sentence. Indeed, she never could think of the Browns without talking Johnson; and, as they were seldom absent from her thoughts just then, I heard many a rolling three-piled sentence.

Now Miss Matty Jenkyns was chary of candles. We had many devices to use as few as possible. In the winter afternoons she would sit knitting for two or three hours; she could do this in the dark, or by fire-light; and when I asked if I might not ring for candles to finish stitching my wristbands, she told me to 'keep blind man's holiday.' They were usually brought in with tea; but we only burnt one at a time. As we lived in constant preparation for a friend who might come in any evening (but who never did), it required some contrivance to keep our two candles of the same length, ready to be lighted, and to look as if we burnt two always. The candles took it in turns; and, whatever we might be talking about or doing, Miss Matty's eyes were habitually fixed upon the candle, ready to jump up and extinguish it, and to light the other before they had become too uneven in length to be restored to equality in the course of the evening.

Cranford by Elizabeth Gaskell

Pocket Money

When some children's pocket money in 1910 was only a farthing
[a quarter of an old penny] a week, a whole penny [less than one
half of 1p] a week was comparative riches, especially with Marks
and Spencer's Penny Bazaar within reach.

I got a penny a week and was passing rich on it – I know people of my age whose weekly pocket money at that time was a farthing. Could you buy *anything* with a farthing? You could indeed, if you shopped around. There were many kinds of sweets to be had at four ounces a penny: 'ju-jubes' pre-eminently, though these I think were simply sugar-coated jelly shapes and not the lozenges of gum-arabic that the modern dictionaries declare them to be. For a farthing you could buy a foot-long strip (one inch wide) of breakable toffee called hanky-panky; or a sherbert dab – a triangular stick of black liquorice poking out of a paper screw of sherbert; or an Ally Sloper's lunch, which was a tiny 'plate of meat and two veg', all made of sugar (Ally Sloper was a comic-strip character); or a toffee-apple; or an ounce of tigernuts – and these now seem to me the oddest confection of them all. I disliked tigernuts very much, both the texture and the almost-sweet tastelessness, but bought and chewed them on Saturdays because a farthing bought more of them than of anything else. In some shops, and occasionally from ice-cream barrows, you could get a farthing drink of sarsaparilla, a bright pink potion made by boiling the dried roots of American *smilax* and alleged to be a tonic, with a number of medicinal properties which the modern world seems able to do without.

What you could buy for a penny was of course far more impressive than all these farthingsworths; and additional pennies were sometimes to be acquired by selling jam-jars to greengrocers (who used them for bottling fruit) and old newspapers to butchers and fishmongers. I was never permitted, as were some enviable boys, to use the family pram for this purpose; I borrowed a soap box on wheels from an obliging neighbour and stacked it with as many jam-jars or newspapers as it would carry. I remember with some bitterness that more than once I had to bring the whole load home again because the market had been saturated before I got going.

With a whole penny to spend, as distinct from a Saturday penny to be spread over a whole week, you could go into Marks and Spencer's Penny Bazaar and pass an agonizing hour of ecstasy, patrolling the display counters with the penny in your hand. These were the ancestors of the modern supermarkets, hypermarkets, jumbomarkets; nothing cost more than a penny, and a high proportion of the counter-space was allotted to toys, dolls, pencils, crayons, drawing and painting books, and sweets. The variety of little tin model vehicles available at a penny seems to me now, as I recall it, simply astounding. Admittedly they were not fitted with clockwork, you had to push them along or run them down the slopes, but they were excellent little models (made, mostly, in Germany) of the motor vehicles then beginning to appear on our roads; and they included, I remember, a 'Vanguard' motor bus and a perfect model of the City of London Police electric ambulances.

London Particulars by C.H. Rolph

Thrift

Thrift ruled in most country households in the 1920s, but especially in this one:

Waste of any kind was frowned on and I opened my eyes daily to a fretwork carving on my bedroom wall spelling out, 'Waste not want not'. If Mother considered any of us had spent money unnecessarily she accused us of 'eating our white bread first'. It seems the Lincolnshire labourers of her childhood had often to be content with dark home-made rye-bread, and the white wheaten leaf was a treat. In our house, nothing was renewed or replaced unless absolutely necessary. Table knives were sharpened and ground down till some resembled daggers. The clock on the mantelpiece only worked with a wad of paper under one side, but it worked. Draughts blew under the kitchen door, but it was said to make the fire burn better, so nothing was done to stop it. When sheets and blankets became holed they were turned sides to middle. When that no longer sufficed, they became bandages, flannels, dusters, and polishers, all carefully hemmed. Personal clothes were handed down from child to child, and I never remember wearing new clothes till I went to Grammar School. Egg shells and broken pottery were pulverised to provide grit for the hens. Goose grease was preserved to rub on the chest against winter coughs, and anoint hands and toes when we had chilblains. All string was husbanded and knots carefully undone. Water buckets with holes became coal buckets; broken metal handles were replaced with cord. Brooms were used down to the last whisker and then used for firewood. Meat bones were hoarded for the rag-and-bone man after the dog had had his picking. When boots finally wore out, tongues and tops were removed to repair harness. Rabbit skins were dried and preserved to make gloves. Household waste went to the pigs. The hens drank their water from chamber pots which had lost their handles. When we killed hens, the soft feathers were used to re-stuff pillows. By such means were 'outgoings' reduced.

A Yeoman Farmer's Son by H. St G. Cramp

The Means Test

Unemployment in the 1930s was dire enough but when a wife and children had to be supported it was also demeaning, for the dreaded Means Test had to be faced.

I recalled a tribunal of the early 1930s. I was married at the time, our two children were infants (Larry a babe in arms) and although I could get a few days of casual work as a coalbagger in the winter, I was mostly unemployed during the summer. I was drawing a weekly sum of twenty-seven shillings and threepence to support us all (fifteen shillings and threepence for myself, eight shillings for my wife, and two shillings for each child – the previous amount having been cut by ten per cent in 1930). This sum had to buy all our food, pay the rent, buy the children's clothes, pay the weekly instalments on furniture, and the numerous small extras – and no matter what anyone hears about money going further in those days, I think it may be said that we did not riot in opulence on it. The government had brought in the Means Test, and this measure was interpreted in a harsh manner by the various tribunals enforcing it in Bolton. Not only were the savings, down to a single pound, of any unemployed person taken into account and his or her unemployment insurance benefit either cut or stopped in lieu of this – a practice that hit the thrifty spinner severely and unfairly – but visits were made to each home by an official, questions were asked of neighbours, and an inspection of furniture and all property was made. Anyone owning disposable articles such as a gold watch, motorcycle, or anything that could be sold was told to sell it, the amount received to serve in place of benefit. The income of every member of the family was taken into account, and deductions in the benefit of those who were unemployed made accordingly. This resulted in the break up of many families, for unemployed sons or daughters left home so as to ensure being entitled to their benefit, and so did fathers of families, men in their fifties or early sixties – many moved backward and forwards between home and lodgings – and young workers went living elsewhere so that the father could apply for the full allowance. Indescribable domestic misery, faction and chaos were created in thousands of what had been relatively happy homes. I was asked various questions about whether I had any money on one side or in the post office savings bank, and did I own anything, had I a motorbike, a watch or anything that could be sold, and which money would help to keep us for a period during which the unemployment pay would be stopped. I was asked about where we lived, and I explained that it was at number 11 Ainscough Street, that we rented two back rooms in the house, shared a kitchen, and that the tenant was a Mr Carr, the husband of a sister of my wife. I explained that he worked for a property repairer, and the eight shillings a week which we paid him helped for a house larger than the usual small cottage. I answered openly and clearly, even to informing them of the new in-law relationship. They turned away and conferred in whispers . . . but the judgement the chairman delivered was that in their civil judicial authority they had reached the conclusion – it was couched in these terms – that the said brother-in-law of my wife should reduce our rent by four shillings per week. 'You're living with your wife's sister's husband,' was how he put it . . . and since he is in work as a property repairer, and considering the state of the economy, and the plight of the country generally, we consider it's only right and proper that he do his share to get us back on our feet by reducing your rent. We therefore make an order that your weekly unemployment may be reduced by the said four shillings from this date on.' I was so taken aback by the decision, and humiliated by the ordeal, that I could only mumble a few mild words of protest.

On the Pig's Back by Bill Naughton

The Way We Worked

Fifteenth-Century Parents and Apprenticeship

Fifteenth-century English parents were not noted for the fondness of their children.

One of the most unflattering glimpses of fifteenth-century English apprenticeship, before the system became structured by statute, is offered by an Italian observer. He notes that:

The want of affection in the English is strongly manifested towards their children; for after having kept them at home till they arrive at the age of 7 or 9 years at the utmost, they put them out, both males and females, to hard service in the houses of other people, binding them generally for another 7 or 9 years. And these are called apprentices, and during that time they perform all the most menial offices; and few are born who are exempted from this fate, for every one, however rich he may be, sends away his children into the houses of others, whilst he, in return, receives those of strangers into his own. And on inquiring the reason for this severity, they answered that they did it in order that their children might learn better manners. But I, for my part, believe that they do it because they like to enjoy all their comforts themselves, and that they are better served by strangers than they would be by their own children. Besides which the English being great epicures, and very avaricious by nature, indulge in the most delicate fare themselves and give their household the coarsest bread, and beer, and cold meat bakes on Sunday for the week. . . . That if they had their own children at home they would be obliged to give them the same food they made use of for themselves. That if the English sent their children away from home to learn virtue and good manners, and took them back again when their apprenticeship was over, they might perhaps be excused; but they never return, for the girls are settled by their patrons, and the boys make the best marriages they can, and assisted by their patrons, not by their father, they also open a house and strive diligently by this means to make some fortune for themselves. . . .

Deloney expressed this attitude best in his ballad of the wool trade where he observed young children picking and sorting wool for the spinners. He marveled that: 'Poor people whom God lightly blessed with most children, did by means of this occupation so order them, that by the time they were come to be six or seven years of age they were able to get their own bread.'

The History of Childhood edited by Lloyd de Mause

Shirtmakers

Thomas Hood (1798–1845) portrays the pitiable plight of the early nineteenth century cottage shirtmakers in his famous poem.

Song of the Shirt

With fingers weary and worn,
With eyelids heavy and red,
A woman sat in unwomanly rags,
Plying her needle and thread—
Stitch—stitch—stitch!
In poverty, hunger, and dirt,
And still with a voice of dolorous pitch
She sang the 'Song of the Shirt.'

'Work—work—work!
While the cock is crowing aloof;
And work—work—work
Till the stars shine through the roof!
It's oh to be a slave
Along with the barbarous Turk,
Where woman has never a soul to save,
If this is Christian work!

'Work—work—work!
Till the brain begins to swim;
Work—work—work!
Till the eyes are heavy and dim,
Seam, and gusset, and band,—
Band, and gusset, and seam,
Till over the buttons I fall asleep,
And sew them on in a dream!

'O men with Sisters dear!
O men with Mothers and Wives!
It is no linen you're wearing out,
But human creatures' lives!
Stitch—stitch—stitch,
In poverty, hunger, and dirt,
Sewing at once, with a double thread,
A Shroud as well as a Shirt!

The Mines and Child Labour

The employment of young children in mines under conditions unthinkable today lasted until 1842.

In May, 1842, four men – Southwood Smith, a doctor, Thomas Tooke an economist, and R. J. Saunders and Leonard Horner, factory inspectors – published a document which profoundly troubled the conscience of England. It was called the First Report of the Children's Employment Commission. It dealt with the conditions of labour of children and young persons working in coal mines. The commission had been set up two years before by Lord Melbourne's government, largely through the pertinacity of Lord Ashley, an inconveniently well-connected young Tory of strong evangelical tendencies who had taken up the cause of the north-country factor operatives with an enthusiasm which seemed to some of his contemporaries to border on the hysterical.

Everybody knew that the conditions of life and labour in the new factory towns of the north and midlands, until now a remote, barren and little visited part of the country, were of a rough and primitive character. There had always been rough and primitive Englishmen, and in these smoky and unsavoury districts they were undoubtedly on the increase. It was part of the price that had to be paid for the nation's growing health. But the revelations of the Commissioners' pages took the country by surprise.

From this document it appeared that the employment of children of seven or eight years old in coal mines was almost universal. In some pits they began work at a still earlier age: a case was even recorded of a child of three. Some were employed as 'trappers,' others for pushing or drawing coal trucks along the pit tunnels. A trapper, who operated the ventilation doors on which the safety of the mines depended, would often spend as many as sixteen hours a day crouching in solitude in a small dark hole.

'Although this employment scarcely deserves the name of labour,' ran the Commission's report, 'yet as the children engaged in it are commonly excluded from light and are always without companions, it would, were it not for the passing and repassing of the coal carriages, amount to solitary confinement of the worst order.'

Those who drew the trucks were 'harnessed like dogs in a go-cart' and crawled on all-fours down passages in some places only eighteen inches high. Other children worked at the pumps in the under-bottom of the pits, standing ankle deep in water for twelve hours. One who was cited, only six years of age, carried or dragged half a hundredweight every day up a distance equivalent to the height of St. Paul's Cathedral.

What struck the conscience of early Victorian England with especial horror was the fact that girls as well as boys were employed in these tasks. Naked to the waist, and with chains drawn between their legs, the future mothers of Englishmen crawled on all-fours down tunnels under the earth drawing Egyptian burdens. Women by the age of 30 were old and infirm cripples. Such labour, degrading all who engaged in it, was often accompanied by debauchery and sickening cruelty: one witness before the Commission described how he had seen a boy beaten with a pick-axe. Lord Ashley in a speech in the Commons mentioned another whose mater was in the habit of thrashing him with a stick through which a nail had been driven: the child's back and loins were beaten to a jelly, his arm was broken and his head covered with the marks of old wounds. To add to its horrors the Report was illustrated with pictures.

Here was something never contemplated by Church and State. 'We in England,' wrote a leading journal, 'have put ourselves forward in every possible way that could savour of ostentation as champions of the whole human race; and we are now, on our own showing, exhibited to the world as empty braggarts and shallow pretenders virtues which we do not possess . . . we have listened to the cries of the slave afar off, but we have shut our ears to the moaning of the slave at our feet.' When Ashley, striking while the iron was hot, rose in the Commons a month later to introduce a Bill excluding all women and girls from the pits and boys under thirteen, he found himself almost a national hero.

English Saga 1840–1940 by Sir Arthur Bryant

The Knocker-up

The knocker-up was a familiar figure in the lives of workers in the nineteenth century and early years of the twentieth centuries.

Old Jimmie Spit-and-Wink, the knocker up, did not wear clogs. Years before, he was standing upon a lorry, and a heavy bolt of cloth, dropped from a warehouse landing several floors above him, missed the usual precision of its throw, and smashed his leg. The leg went, and Jimmie's job went, and his nerves went, leaving him with the melancholy affliction that gave him his nickname. The whole side of his face would jerk his eye into a wink, and, as if by reflex action, he would then automatically spit.

They gave him a wooden leg, and on his other foot he wore a big, hobnailed boot, not a clog. For as long as most people could remember, he had been knocker-up, spitting and winking through the morning with none to see him, carrying his little bunch of wires upon a pole, and playing with this a tattoo upon the windows of his clientele.

In the stillness the rattle of Jimmie's wires on the windows could be heard, and the shrill sound of the witticisms which cheered himself and his victims.

'Come on theer, Mrs Hannaway. Buzzer'll be goin' afore thee's got this corsets on. Never mind *what* thee's doing'. There's bairns enough in t'world already.'

Then off he went, *thud-clatter, thud-clatter,* down the empty street, punctuating the darkness with that raucous clearing of the throat that preceded expectoration.

Fame is the Spur by Howard Spring

Riches

In 1912 £2.50 per week was half-way to riches for the young Neville Cardus.

As usual whenever I have been stranded at crossroads, with no signposts to help an instinctive feeling of the way, a miracle happened. One day, I picked up a sporting newspaper called the *Athletic News*; I did not ever read sporting periodicals and I don't think I had ever seen this particular journal until, one Monday morning in January 1912, I somehow found myself turnings its pages and hit upon an advertisement: 'Wanted assistant Cricket Coach at Shrewsbury School. Must be good bowler. Apply with testimonials, etc.'

I was then a fairly good bowler, slow to medium, with an off-break. I applied for the job. Weeks went by and no reply came. I forgot all about it. One night I went to hear *Tristan and Isolde* at the Theatre Royal in Manchester; I climbed up a Piranesi stairway to the high gallery and the music came to me like the sound of a rising sea. I walked home to my lodgings; four miles through dank and squalor, my mind and heart aching with Isolde's 'So bange Tage.' When I got into the house and turned on the light (everybody was asleep), I saw a letter for me on the chest of drawers. It bore the Shrewsbury crest and motto: Intus Si Recte Ne Labora. I was offered the post of assistant professional coach at the salary of two pounds ten weekly; and the term would begin in the first week of May and extend to the last week of July. I at once glimpsed that the chance of my life had come. I could live at Shrewsbury on a pound a week and put the rest into the post office savings bank. By the end of the term I would have accumulated at least £18. I would have capital on which to fall back when summer had gone and I had to return to Manchester. Why, with £18 I would safely be able to launch into literature and music as a full-time winter study and occupation!

You can measure from this decision of young Cardus what bliss it was to be alive then; the very thought of £18 in my possession in one lump sum, for which you could if you chose receive golden sovereigns, was strength and fortification. Yet to this day I am surprised that I was bold enough to venture into a strange world. Remember, I had never journeyed far beyond Manchester and I was one of the shyest and most self-conscious of youths, one of those who when they went into a Lyons café (I never aspired to restaurants) sat down on the seat nearest the door; if a waitress looked at me as I was peering into the café I would not dare to enter at all. Mr. Kipps was like that. Today I regard my decision to uproot myself from Manchester, to break with the environment and habits of a groping lifetime, to go alone into a new social habitat 'amongst the nobs' (as the socialists told me they would be: also they said I was backsliding), to face the critical gaze of an English public school and, most awful of all, to have my work inspected by a famous All-England cricketer who would be my boss – here were faith and foolhardiness to which I am sure I could not rise at the present time, in the same circumstances.

Autobiography by Sir Neville Cardus

LYONS CAFÉ

THEATRE ROYAL
MANCHESTER
Tristan
&
Isolde
RICHARD WAGNER
January 1912

ATHLETICS NEWS
CRICKET COACH
WANTED
AT
SHREWSBURY
SCHOOL
£2.10S per week

Boots

Life in service at a house in Adelaide Crescent, Hove, in the 1920s, the home of the Reverend Clydesdale, his wife and small daughter, was trying in the extreme. The house was staffed by a butler, a cook, a parlour maid, two housemaids, a kitchen maid, a governess and a gardener/chauffeur.

In my first months there I made one mistake after another. I particularly remember one day when I was doing the front door – I was a bit late this particular morning – the newsboy came with the papers. As I went to put them on the hall table, Mrs Clydesdale came down the stairs. I went to hand her the papers. She looked at me as if I were something sub-human. She didn't speak a word, she just stood there looking at me as though she could hardly believe that someone like me could be walking and breathing. I thought, what's the matter? I've got my cap on, I've got my apron on, I've got by black stockings and shoes; I couldn't think what was wrong. Then at last she spoke. She said, 'Langley, never, never on any occasion ever hand anything to me in your bare hands, always use a silver salver. Surely you know better than that,' she said. 'Your mother was in service, didn't she teach you anything?' I thought it was terrible. Tears started to trickle down my cheeks; that someone could think that you were so low that you couldn't even hand them anything out of your hands without it first being placed on a silver salver.

I was so miserable about this that I wanted to go home; it seemed the last straw. I thought, I can't stand domestic service. I don't think I ever felt so wretched before or after that. But I knew I couldn't go home, because we had only three rooms – we lived in the bottom half of a house, two rooms on the ground floor and one in the middle – and since I had come into service, my mother's father had died, and my grandmother had to come and live with us. So now there just wasn't room. I didn't even say anything to my mother about it. What was the good of making them unhappy as well? In any case I think she'd just have said, 'Take no notice.' She'd have been right. That's what you had to do if you wanted to keep any pride at all – just take no notice.

Up I got at five-thirty, dragged myself downstairs, and presented myself to the kitchen range. I lit it, cleaned it, and lit the fire in the servants' hall.

Then I'd tear upstairs to do the front door, which was all white paint and brass – a thankless task, particularly in the winter, for when I'd got it all bright and sunny the wind from the sea tarnished it again. So by the time Madam saw it, it was something to find fault with.

Then there were fourteen wide stone steps to be scrubbed. Back downstairs again, and there was Mary waiting with all the boots and shoes.

I remember the first morning. She said, 'Carrie' (that was the head housemaid) 'says she hopes you know how to clean boots and shoes.' 'Well, of course I do,' I said. After all, I'd done them at home. But I didn't know how to do them the way they wanted them done.

The Reverend, he used to wear boots all day; black boots in the week and brown boots on Sundays. In the evenings he changed into black patent shoes. Madam wore black or brown, often both during the course of the day. Then there were the governess's, and Leonora's. These I did and I thought they looked very nice indeed. Well, the toes shone anyway.

When Mary came down for them she said, 'Oh, they won't do. They won't do at all.' I said, 'What's the matter with them? They look all right to me.' 'All right,' she said, 'I'll take them up if you like but Carrie will only sling them back at me.'

About two minutes afterwards down she came again and said, 'It's like I said, they won't do. You haven't done the insteps.' 'The insteps?' I said. 'I never knew you had to clean underneath the shoes.' So I did that, gave them another polish, and Mary took them up again.

Seconds later back she came and said, 'You haven't done the bootlaces.' I said, 'Haven't done the bootlaces!' 'Don't you know?' she said. 'You have to iron all the bootlaces, take them all out and iron them.' I thought she was joking. 'Iron the bootlaces?' I said. She said, 'Yes.' You see in those days they weren't the narrow little bootlaces they are now, they were quite half an inch wide. In fact Mrs Clydesdale's and Leonora's were nearly an inch wide.

So I had to take the laces out of the shoes and iron them. Of course, there were no electric irons, just flat irons. They had to be heated in front of the fire, and that took nearly a quarter of an hour. Never in all my life have I seen such a footling procedure.

Below Stairs by Margaret Powell

Hiring Fairs

Hiring fairs, where children who had left school would stand at appointed places for prospective employers to examine and interrogate them, were still in existence in the north of England in the 1930s.

I was brought up in a pit village near Bishop Auckland and I never knew my father. He was a miner and he went off to the First World War and got killed. I only knew my mother and grandmother and life was not easy – we often went hungry. When I was a schoolgirl some friends took me on a farm and I used to watch the milking and think what a grand life it was, so healthy, not at all like life in the pits and the factories. By the time I was fourteen I couldn't wait to get away from that place and my mother took me to the hiring fair in the marketplace in Bishop Auckland. The year was 1931 and there were a lot of other lads and lassies standing around anxiously like me. All the farmers stood apart in groups, looking around. Anyway, this man came up to where I was standing with my mother, and asked if I was for hire. I said yes, that I wanted a farm place, and he asked me if I had any experience. I told him that I had watched cows being milked – that was all – but I liked the look of it. He must have liked the look of me because after a bit more discussion he said, 'Well, we'll have to learn you to milk, and learn you to feed calves and the rest will follow on. Here's your God's Penny'. Then he gave me half a crown. I nearly fell through the floor because I didn't know what owning such a lot of money was like before.

They paid me five shillings a week, which was a lot more than most got. I heard the story of a lad, from the Bishop Auckland area like me, who worked at a farm in Teesdale for two shillings and sixpence a week. But the time came when he reached the age when the farmer had to pay sixpence a week for his insurance stamp, and he was sent back home because the man said he couldn't afford it. After a while, the lad turned up back at the farm and offered to work for two shillings and pay his own insurance stamp. When he'd arrived home there had been nothing to eat and not even a bed of his own. That's how it was for lots of families in those days.

I will always maintain that I had a good time in service, and from what I heard there weren't many bad places in the Teesdale area – just the odd one here and there. But they said that it was a different matter over in the west, around Appleby way, where they generally paid more money but worked you very hard and gave you little meat. They told some awful stories about going hungry, no privileges, putting the fire out at six o'clock at night. In winter it go so cold that you would have to wear your clothes in bed.

No, I was well treated, although the hours were long.

I just got Saturday and Sunday nights off, and it would be chapel on a Sunday of course. There was a general rule that lads could stay out until ten o'clock on their night off, but lassies had to be back at 9.30.

Once or twice a year I would go home for a weekend to see my mother.

Daughter of the Dales by Hannah Hauxwell

Handwriting

The days of the quill pen and pride in handwriting are recalled and their passing much regretted.

Before I leave Mr Scaife and Jeeves and the B&FBC (the strange device that was emblazoned in gilt lettering on the leather covers of all its account books), I have to recall that he was the last man but one whom I ever saw writing with a quill pen. The last one was Sir Henry Dickens, KC, Common Serjeant at the Old Bailey in the 1930s, who maddened everyone in Court No. 3 by using an extra large, ultra squeaky and slow-moving quill with which to make his judge's notes during every trial. A much-loved man, dear old Sir Henry Dickens, then in his eighties; but the quill pen was beloved only by visiting antiquarians and Americans, who adored it. Mr Scaife was a real penman. His handwriting, which may still, I suppose, be open to reverent inspection at the Queen Victoria Street offices of what is now more simply called The Bible Society, was to me of an importance second only to Jeeves; for I assiduously copied it – and I dare to think that I was soon doing it quite well.

There are people who attribute the disappearance of handwriting (for it is all but dead) to the arrival of the ballpoint pen. Older grumblers blame the fountain-pen. I can report that as late as 1921 we clerks were not allowed to use fountain-pens. They took the character out of writing, we were told. They also leaked and made a mess of books, papers, fingers, clothes, and handbags. You could pay £25 for a fountain-pen, and you could get one for a shilling (it was called a 'Blackbird'). The posh one was 'self-filling', which meant that you filled it yourself. You replenished its internal bladder with ink by raising a little lever (which normally rested along the side of the pen) with your fingernail, thus closing the bladder and expelling all the air. You then submerged the nib in a bottle of ink, sometimes knocking the whole thing over, and by pressing the little lever back into place you slowly opened the bladder and sucked the ink into it. What, by comparison, was not self-filling was the kind of pen which came with a little glass dropper, a kind of syringe topped with a depressible rubber bulb. The top halves of such pens screwed off so that the fresh ink could be squired in. Lack of squirting experience led to many mishaps.

No employer I worked for would countenance any of this. Pens were intended to renew their ink by being dipped into little pots, ink-wells; but sometimes the pots were embedded in large containers with a base as big as a dinner-plate, whose purpose was to reduce the danger of being knocked over. We were all dippers. (I still know dippers, though I sometimes wonder where they manage to find their ink-wells when they have the misfortune to break or lose them.) But at the risk of sounding like a growling reactionary I shall maintain that the dippers were always better writers than the wielders of fountain-pens, even of those exquisitely refined things which in recent years have been advertised as writing instruments . . . and as I write this, the newspapers have just published (22 September 1984) photographs of the infant Prince Henry's birth certificate, on which the handwriting is totally illegible; and people have been writing to the editors asking what on earth has happened to both loyalty and calligraphy. The loyalty was much in evidence for other reasons and in other ways, but the calligraphy had gone . . . for ever? Not yet, I believe. There is a Society of Scribes and Illuminators and there is a Society for Italic Handwriting, and between them they may yet save one of the bench-marks of civilization.

Further Particulars by C.H. Rolph

The Way We Played

Archery

Archery, besides being a favourite pastime, was a vital component in England's military might and Queen Elizabeth I honoured archery practice with her presence.

The next afternoon, the last day of her stay in Oxford the Queen attended archery practice in Beaumont Fields.

Under a blazing blue sky scholars and citizens alike poured out of North Gate, swung to their left along the narrow lane beside the city wall, then to their right into Beaumont Fields. The scholars who carried bows, and who were to shoot before the Queen, were all very eager and excited, and a little strained, for this was a very great occasion. Archery was still tremendously important, even though the hand-gun was now taking the place of the long-bow in modern warfare. You were no true Englishman if you could not shoot a straight arrow from your bow, and to be watched by the Queen of England while you tried to do it was enough to turn the hottest blood to water and the stoutest heart to a mere pulp. Even Nicholas was flustered as he made his way out of North Gate, with Faithful behind him carrying his bow and arrows.

But at the butts under the palace wall there was a scene of eager activity. The seats of the spectators stretched the length of the wall, with a raised dais for the Queen in the centre, and were already full; dons and scholars, stout merchants and their wives, and apprentices, all in their gayest clothes. They were an audience whose comments never lacked ribaldry or point and under their scrutiny the groups of archers, waiting at each end of the butts for the arrival of the Queen, shifted nervously from foot to foot.

As each man's turn came he had to shoot from first one end and then the other, alternately, so that he should not get set in one position. In this continual flying of arrows in different directions there was a certain amount of danger, but according to the regulations if a man cried out 'Fast!' before he shot he was not held responsible for the injury or death of anyone he might wound or kill. . . . The accident was unfortunate but quite in order. . . . A really expert English bowman could shoot ten arrows in a minute, with a range of two hundred yards, an Henry the Eighth had ordained that no person who had reached the age of twenty-four should shoot at any mark at less than two hundred and twenty yards distant.

So two hundred and twenty yards was the distance between the two wooden discs set up at either end of the space by the palace wall.

In the distance a fanfare of trumpets sounded. The Queen was leaving St. John's, the beautiful College built in a grove of elm trees outside the city wall, where she had that morning been entertained and feasted by its dons. The sound of the cheering grew louder as she came nearer, growing into a roar as the royal party came into the Fields and mounted the steps to the dais. . . . But the groups of waiting archers did not cheer, for their tongues stuck most distressingly to the roofs of their mouths. They straightened themselves, gripped their bows with tense fingers and swallowed hard.

The trumpet sounded again, the murmur of voices died away into silence, and Faithful's sudden depression fell away from him like a black cloak as the figure of a straight young archer stepped forward, brilliant in sunshine, his body laid on his great bow, drawing not with the strength of the arm but with the strength of the body, as Englishmen were taught to do.

As one after the other the figures of the archers took their posts, at the sound of the drawn bowstrings and the sight of the arrows speeding through the air, a queer exultation seized hold of the whole company, consciousness was heightened and imagination took wing. For it was true that the voice of France could be heard in the sound of the trumpets, that preserved the echoes of the horn of Roland, it was equally true that the voice of England was heard in the music of archery, in the humming of the bowstrings, that was like the sound of a plucked harp, and the singing of the arrows in the air. It was a music that was full of memories; of Crécy and the Black Prince, of Agincourt and Harry the Fifth. And not only their music but the bows and arrows themselves carried one back through time; the bows nearly as tall as a man, made of the wood of English yew trees, the descendants of the sacred yews that the Druids had planted round their holy places before the Romans came, the bow-strings of flax from English fields, and the arrows of birch wood feathered from the wings of grey geese. Over and over again, in battle after battle, had those grey geese, flying out from the forests of bent yew, carried death upon their wings. For only Englishmen could use the longbow. Foreigners could never get the knack of it. It was something that Englishmen, yeomen and gentry alike, had to practise from their boyhood up in the butts that stretched behind every village churchyard, sweating over it while the old churchyard yews that had made the bows leapt over the wall to watch, and the grey geese that had feathered the arrows cackled approval up and down the village street. Agincourt had been won by the whole of England, by the yeomen, the yew trees, the grey geese and the fields of flax. The young archer who dazzled Faithful's eyes as he stood in the sunshine was a symbolic figure to the whole of that excited crowd. They thrilled with pride as they looked at him, but they were sad too. He stood for the fast-dying days when a man fighting for his country could feel himself something of an artist and not solely a butcher, and for a voice of England that would soon be stilled. . . . When the last archer had sped the last arrow to its mark a sigh went up from Beaumont Fields, and then silence before the trumpets spoke again and the Queen stepped down from her dais.

Towers in the Mist by Elizabeth Goudge

Boxing

Boxing in 1860 was a brutal bare-knuckle fight to the finish.

Strength and endurance were still the virtues that England, rustic or urban, prized above all others. In April, 1860, on a lovely spring morning, Tom Sayers, the English champion, met Heenan, the American, known to the fancy as the Benicia Boy, on the edge of a wood near Farnborough to fight for the championship of the world. For weeks in every town and village in the land men and women had canvassed the chances of the event, and the police, fearing a fatal casualty in those days of timeless contests and bare fists, had forbidden the fight and kept close watch on the would-be combatants. But where there was a will there was a way; old England was not to be disappointed. On the night before the great day every tavern and public-house in London remained open all night until the word went round where the trains to the secret ringside were to start.

Sayers was thirty-four, stood five foot eight, and weighed ten stone twelve. His American challenger was eight years younger, stood five inches taller and weighed thirteen stone. In the opening rounds the Englishman was knocked down repeatedly, only to rise smiling for more. The blood poured down his brown, tanned face which shone in the morning sun as though it had been carved of old oak. For two hours after his right arm was broken by a terrific blow of Heenan's he fought on, and, when the police broke through the exultant crowed into the ring, the English champion, giving as good as he took, was still undefeated.

English Saga 1840–1940 by Sir Arthur Bryant

The Boat Race

Time was when the Oxford and Cambridge Boat Race gripped the nation and partisanship extended far beyond the two universities and the inhabitants of the Thames riverside between Putney and Mortlake.

This event has divided the British into Dark Blues and Light Blues ever since it became an annual contest in 1856 (it was started in 1829); but I doubt that the sale of blue lapel badges and streamers reached the same frenzied level anywhere as in Putney and Fulham when I was a boy. Almost everyone seemed to wear, on the day, a light or dark blue enamelled lapel badge or button; and I knew of syndicates of boys who spread themselves out along the Putney-to-Mortlake towpath, not so much to watch the boat race as to solicit people's badges and buttons once it was over.

'Want yer badge any more Guv'nor?' 'Give us yer badge,' they would wheedle; and, if their timing was right, they got badges by the score. Collectively they got badges by the thousand, most of them being put away until the following year, for re-sale to the boat-race public as if they were brand new. Today I see my own share in this enterprise as one of the feebler commercial efforts in a signally uncommercial life, for although I joined enthusiastically in the business of soliciting *post facto* badges from riverside Oxford and Cambridge supporters, I gave them away almost at once to boys who were collecting them in greater earnestness, and who used large shopping bags for the purpose.

Anyway the boat race was a Great Annual Event, sustaining fierce antagonisms and much jeering, sometimes (indeed I think usually) dividing families, sometimes leading to fights; and with my co-urchins I always spent the whole day, with a packed lunch, somewhere on the towpath between Putney and Hammersmith bridges. In 1912, on a cold and windy 30 March, both boats filled with water and the Cambridge one sank. The Oxford crew, to my great joy as one of their supporters, got out in shallow water, emptied out their boat, and went on to complete the course. Alas, the umpires decided that it was 'no race'. It was re-rowed on 1 April and Oxford won by three lengths. My brother Harold supported Cambridge, for no better reason, I believe, than his scholarship examination was the 'Cambridge Junior Local'; and this sinking of the Cambridge boat was eclipsed, for him, only by the sinking of the *Titanic* a fortnight later.

London Particulars by C.H. Rolph

Marriage of Convenience

In 1921 marriage was conveniently fitted into the working day of a cricket writer for the Manchester Guardian.

There are many things about cricket, apart from the skill and the score. There is, first of all, the leisure to do something else. Cricket, like music, has its slow movements, especially when my native county of Lancashire is batting. I married the good companion who is my wife during a Lancashire innings. The event occurred in June, 1921; I went as usual to Old Trafford, stayed for a while and saw Hallows and Makepeace come forth to bat. As usual they opened with care. Then I had to leave, had to take a taxi to Manchester, there to be joined in wedlock at a registry office. Then I – that is, we – returned to Old Trafford. While I had been away from the match and had committed the most responsible and irrevocable act in mortal man's life, Lancashire had increased their total by exactly seventeen – Makepeace 5, Hallows 11, and one leg-bye.

Autobiography by Sir Neville Cardus

What We Ate and What We Wore

Ceremony at Mealtimes

In the days when servants were plentiful ceremony played a large part in the serving of meals both upstairs and downstairs.

In late medieval and Tudor households, the ceremony involved in serving up meals is almost unbelievable. Even the minor business of supplying an earl with a bedside snack for the night involved ten servants in a ritual of bowing, kissing and processing all over the house. By the eighteenth century ritual had largely disappeared; but vestiges survived into Edwardian days, as in the dinner procession of upper servants from servants' hall to housekeeper's room. In general, the self-importance of upper servants derived from the fact that their predecessors had once been gentry.

A Country House Companion by Mark Girouard

The Country Gentleman's Food

Country gentry in the eighteenth century fared lavishly.

The big landowners lived exceeding well. Their farms, orchards and kitchen gardens supplied them with a wealth of food to which they added costly wines and other luxuries from abroad.

Breakfast, usually a light meal of tea, coffee or chocolate, with rusks or cakes, was taken at 9 or 10 o'clock and was followed an hour or so later by a glass of sherry and a biscuit. In the early part of the century dinner was eaten about 2 p.m. but the hour tended to get later and later until by about 1780 it was not uncommon for the squire and his guests to sit down to their chief meal at 3 or even 4 in the afternoon.

The following description of what appears to have been a quite ordinary dinner is taken from Catharine Hutton's letters:

A little before three, we sat down to dinner, which consisted of three boiled chickens at top, a very fine haunch of venison at bottom; ham on one side, a flour pudding on the other, and beans in the middle. After the cloth was removed, we had gooseberries, and a remarkably fine dish of apricots.

It was by no means an unusual dinner that the Rev. James Woodforde gave to Mrs Farr on April 19th, 1768:

A roasted Shoulder of Mutton and a plum Pudding – Veal Cutlets, Frill'd Potatoes, cold Tongue, Ham and cold roast Beef, and eggs in their shells. Punch, Wine, Beer and Cyder for drinking.

It was a very different matter when he gave an 'elegant' dinner, as he did to a party of friends on April 20th, 1774.

The first course was, part of a large Cod, a Chine of Mutton, some Soup, a Chicken Pye, Puddings and Roots, etc. Second course, Pidgeons and Asparagus. A Fillet of Veal with Mushrooms and high Sauce with it, rosted

Sweetbreads, hot Lobster, Apricot Tart and in the Middle a Pyramid of Syllabubs and Jellies. We had Dessert of Fruit after Dinner, and Madeira, White Port and red to drink as Wine.

It seems unnecessary for him to add 'We were all very cheerful and merry'.

Sometimes the country gentry followed the town fashion of drinking tea at 5 or 6 o'clock, but more often they sat over their dinner for several hours. Supper, which usually consisted of a variety of cold meats, was seldom eaten before 10 p.m. These people were prodigious meat eaters, and consumed correspondingly small amounts of bread.

The Englishman's Food: Five Centuries of English Diet by Drummond and Wilbraham

Goody

*The simple and universal dish of bread and milk could sometimes
be made into a culinary creation which in rural Ireland was given
a special name and savoured as a source of consolation by both old
and young.*

Goody was a balm to bruised minds and bodies and held a special place in
all our hearts. Mothers made it when we were feeling sick, but not sick
enough for medicine and definitely not needing the doctor – maybe
feeling just a little out of step with our fellow human beings and in need
of loving or the knowledge that somebody loved us. It was a simple but
effective antidote to all ills and was within the scope of all budgets.

Tufts of white bread were plucked from a thick cut or a well-padded
heel of a loaf to line the bottom of a cup or a basin, depending on the size
of the consumer. Some dressers boasted a colourful, flowery basin which
was reserved especially for making goody. On top of the foundation layer
of bread came a generous shake of sugar, and sweet-toothed people turned
the sugar bowl sideways and poured freely. Then another covering of
bread was added, and more sugar, and so on, layer upon layer until it rose,
dome-like, over the rim.

While this tiered miracle was being created a wary eye was kept on a
saucepan of milk heating on a rake-out of hot coals by the fire. You forgot
it at your peril; if you took your eye off it for one second it could erupt in
billowing bubbles and overflow on to the fire, scattering ashes and filling
the kitchen with an acrid smell. Experienced goody makers managed to
get the two jobs to reach completion simultaneously. Then the boiling
milk was poured gently in circular motion over the soft, spongy bread and
sugar, which sank with a subdued sigh beneath the scalding waterfall.
Some discerning people like to hold back the skim at the top of the milk,
which might be flecked with turf dust and ashes, while other, less

fastidious souls let it all pour in. Then, with a big spoon, the entire concoction was squelched up and down, the spoon making a slurping passage through the goody to meet the bottom of the bowl with a dull thud. As the mixing progressed the goody cooled and the connoisseur knew when the precise point for satisfying expectant taste-buds had been reached. Thus was created a soft, sweet, creamy bowl of delicious, slushy sedation.

With this soothing seductive mush babies were weaned off the breast and introduced to solid food. In later years the goody was there when no other comfort was available. Many a hardened bachelor, long in the tooth, coming home on a cold day from the fair and having no welcoming arms to erase the memory of a bad bargain, found his solace in a basin of hot goody. His blood chilled by a long trudge up a mountainy road with a cold wind whipping around his ears, he was rejuvenated and reheated by this bowl of warm comfort. Often an overly discerning lady, unwilling to wrinkle her linen sheets with what she considered the unsuitable manhood available, took a china cup of consoling goody to see her through the night. Happy couples, too, having bedded down their young after a hectic day, shared a bowl of warm goody before going on to share greater comforts. Then, in old age, when sensitive molars could send searing pain through brittle jaws, goody gently weaned them off solid fare with its delicate touch.

Chewing, which rocked unsteady teeth in their shrunken rooting ground, was no longer necessary as goody slid effortlessly over flawed masticators.

Goody was a source of consolation for all seasons. It was an infantile soother, a male menopause stress-reliever, a female oestrogen replacer and, in old age, the last comfort against the ravages of time.

To School through the Fields by Alice Taylor

Children's Clothing

Children's clothes, especially boys', in Victorian times seems grotesque today.

Many Victorian children had too much rather than too little clothing. Few parents noticed what Charles Kingsley pointed out, the instinct of children to get rid of clothes and to cuddle to flesh. Instead they were trained from infancy never to expose themselves. When little girls began to walk they were put into a vest, a chemise – without which it was not 'nice' to go – and stays. Both sexes wore stays, boys till about seven, girls for a lifetime. There were buttons to hold up garters, drawers, the flannel petticoat, the white petticoat with its bodice, black stockings, a frock and pinafore. Boys began with the same set of dresses, but it was a great day when one got his first breeches (though the experience was supposed to be a trauma for his mother).

> Joy to Philip! he this day
> Has his long coats cast away,
> And, (the childish season gone)
> Puts the manly breeches on. . . .
> Sashes, frocks to those that need 'em,
> Philip's limbs have got their freedom.
> He can run, or he can ride,
> And do twenty things beside
> Which his petticoats forbad:
> Is he not a happy lad?

One cannot help wondering if girls ever had such a moment of joy.

The History of Childhood edited by Lloyd de Mause

Caps

Time was when practically every boy and every man wore a cap.

The author is writing of his childhood in Bolton in the 1920s.

Every single one in the backstreet, from the youngest to the oldest, with the sole exception of myself, wears a cap. They cannot understand why I go around bareheaded, especially in the rain, and seem to put it down to my being Irish and not knowing any better. The cloth cap – the adjective never heard among those who wear such – is an indispensable item of dress. It is worn by every male from the age of five until death; almost literally so in certain cases, for when I go errands for Mrs Hardman I often see Mr Hardman sat up in bed in the front kitchen – he suffers from bronchitis and the upstairs bedroom is too cold – with his cap on. A cap worn for such long periods – as in the case of spectacles – becomes closely identified with the face, and often there is an astonishing change when the headgear is removed. Just as wire spectacles produce a furrow across the bridge of the nose, the constant wearing of a heavy cap brings about a decided groove around the lower part of the head of the wearer, and also flattens the hair. These caps are bulky, bulging out an inch or two at the side, with huge nebs at the front which protrude over the forehead. The cap on your head tells a lot about you: your job, of course – the greasy cap of the mill worker distinct from that of the miner – but also your personality and character, what you are and what you would like others to think you are. The timid child will want to pull down his cap at the front, whilst the bolder child will cock it back a bit – and with variations these traits will persist throughout life. The average male would as soon go out of the front door without trousers as without his cap; 'I feel undressed without mi cap,' or 'I'm lost without a cap,' is often heard. Even in the tidy homes caps rate a place on the dresser, mostly over an ornament, the heads of bronze horses being a regular hanging place; Dad has the favourite place, the horse's head nearest the door, and each member of the family his own place in order of seniority downwards.

Saintly Billy by Bill Naughton

What We Learned

The Canon's Children

How the numerous children of Canon Leigh, of Christchurch, Oxford, were educated in 1572. Will and Thomas were nine and eight, Joyeuce and Grace were older and the twins younger.

There was a constant patter of feet on the path under the window, and a succession of flying figures crossing the quadrangle, for work began at six and scholars were hurrying to their lectures. Great Tom boomed out the hour from the Cathedral tower and Canon Leigh set the twins hastily upon the floor and hurried into the study to fetch the books he needed for his six o'clock lecture.

Sighing, and wiping their mouths with the backs of their hands, Will and Thomas slid to the floor and got their school books from the chest under the window, just as Dorothy entered from the kitchen with their dinners in little leather bags. They attended the grammar school at Queen's College, where they went every morning at six o'clock, returning at five-thirty in the evening. Of this eleven hours' working day, two hours, eleven to one, were free for eating the dinners of cold meat and bread that they had brought with them, and for shooting at the butts, but the rest of the time was devoted to grammar, logic, rhetoric, arithmetic, music, geometry and astronomy.

> 'Tis Grammar teaches how to speak,
> And Logic sifts the false from true;
> By Rhetoric we learn to deck
> Each word with its own proper hue.
> Arithmetic of number treats,
> And Music rules the Church's praise;
> Geometry the round earth meets,
> Astronomy the starry ways.

They had holidays, of course, eighteen days at Christmas, twelve at Easter and nine at Whitsuntide, but it was extraordinary how quickly they seemed to pass . . . They envied the twins, who stayed at home and were taught by Great-Aunt.

Not that the twins envied themselves. Joyeuce and Grace had long ago learnt all of the little that Great-Aunt knew and Grace now helped Joyeuce in the work of the house, so the twins and Diccon received Great-Aunt's instructions in solitary glory, and it was awful.

As they stood at the front door, seeing the men of the family off to work, their hearts sank down and down. . . . Oh, if only they were grown up, or men, or dead, or anything so that they need not receive instruction from Dame Susan Cholmeley. . . But it would be best of all to be grown up.

Towers in the Mist by Elizabeth Goudge

Oxford Scholars

End of term at Oxford in the time of Elizabeth I was a special time.

The long summer holidays, arranged to suit the harvesting, were upon them. All the scholars must go home, rich and poor alike, to help gather in the corn and the wheat and the barley that were clothing England in a robe of green and gold and orange-tawny that bent before the wind under a sky of burning blue.

The day when the scholars departed was a great day. Travelling in companies as protection against rogues and vagabonds they passed out north, south, east and west through the gates of the city, singing and laughing and shouting out final insults at the townspeople who thronged the streets to see them go.

Some evil imps of the town had mounted the belfries and rang out peals of thanksgiving as the companies wended their way past the guardian towers.

'At North Gate and South Gate, too, Saint Michael guards the way,
While o'er the East and o'er the West Saint Peter holds his sway.'

Some of the scholars chanted the old rhyme and looked up at the towers as they passed beneath them; some of them glad to be going, some of them sorry, and some of the older ones heartbroken because their time at Oxford was over and they would never come back again except as the old fogeys of the past.

The rich scholars, the noblemen and squires' sons, rode on horseback with their mounted servants clattering behind them; they would put up at the fine houses of friends and relatives and they had their best clothes with them in saddle bags; their friends would give them fresh horses and they would be home in no time. But the poor scholars had to walk, sleeping under hedges if the weather was fine or at the rough inns if it was wet, and it would be a long time before they got to their journey's end, with their faces brown as berries and their shoes worn through.

[It was even worse at Christmas when] not every scholar could go home. Rich men who could afford horses, or who had hospitable friends near at hand, could leave Oxford, but for poor men who lived a long way off, the journey over roads knee-deep in mire would have been interminable; they would no sooner have got there than they would have to come back again.

Towers in the Mist by Elizabeth Goodge

An Orphan with Academic Ambitions

A fourteen-year-old orphan fallen on bad times during the reign of Elizabeth I is still determined to be a scholar and to go to Oxford.

. . . He was still himself, Faithful Croker. He wiped his nose on the back of his hand and had a good look at as much of himself as he was able to see, and the sight was not reassuring. His jerkin, made of coarse brown frieze, was dirty, and so torn that his elbows showed through the holes, and as for his shoes, he had walked them to pieces and they were kept in place on his swollen, bruised feet by strips of dirty rag. It was many weeks since he and a looking-glass had come face to face, but it was too much to hope that there had been any change for the better between then and now, and it was with gloom that he recollected what he had last seen. . . . A boy of fourteen with a head far too large for the puny body it was set upon, a round face pitted with smallpox, a snub nose, a large mouth with a front tooth missing, and a shock of rough, dust-coloured hair that stuck out in plumes over the large ears, that did not lie flat against the head but projected at the side in a very distressing manner. Would Oxford, when this creature presented itself at the gates of the city, be impressed? . . . Faithful feared not.

From gloomy consideration of his personal appearance Faithful let his thoughts slip back over his equally disreputable past. It held, he felt, only one qualification that fitted him to present himself at the city down below, and that was his passionate love of learning. He had pursued it from his cradle. He had been hitting his nurse over the head with a horn book, so said his father, at an age when most infants were brandishing rattles, and he could lisp out sentences from Virgil when other children were still entangled in their A B C. When as a small boy he became a scholar at Saint Paul's, Westminster, where his father was a master, he was hailed as a prodigy, and his path seemed to stretch straight and easy before him, winding over hill and dale to Oxford, that goal of pilgrimage to which came rich men, poor men, saints and sinners to drink deep of the well of learning. . . . Or at least so thought Faithful, ignorant as yet how many other things could be drunk deep of within the walls of the city of dreams.

But poor Faithful had no luck, for his father, an improvident and tiresome person who had already done Faithful an injury by giving him for a mother a slut out of the streets whom he had not bothered to marry, now got himself dismissed for petty theft and then died, leaving Faithful entirely alone in the world and with no possessions at all except his clothes, a cat, his father's Virgil and a tattered copy of Foxe's *Book of Martyrs*. Faithful's subsequent adventures would have filled an entire book. He, the cat, Virgil and the Martyrs went on the streets together and proceeded to pick a living as best they could. The cat who, like all cats, with a snob, soon decided to better herself and took service with an alderman, but Virgil and the Martyrs, hung round his neck in a bag, stuck to Faithful, and together they washed pots at taverns, swept chimneys, cleaned windows and carted garbage. At one time they fell in with a performing dog and ran a little theatrical performance of their own with him; Faithful standing on his head with Virgil balanced on his feet and the dog standing on his hind legs with the Martyrs balanced on his nose. Another time they, like Shakespeare in his bad days, were employed to hold the horses outside a genuine theatre; but the poor dog got kicked and died of it and Faithful had not the heart to go on. Yet he did not become embittered by these experiences; on the contrary they did him good. His great gift, that peacefulness that could create an oasis of calm about himself and other people wherever he might be, stood him in good stead even when stuck half way up a chimney, and his amazing intellect fed itself on every experience that came his way. But nevertheless he was not contented. He still wanted above all things to be a scholar and go to Oxford, and standing on his head in the street did not seem likely to get him there.

Towers in the Mist by Elizabeth Goodge

School Discipline

Harsh discipline was the norm for both grammar school pupils and apprentices in the seventeenth century.

Certainly the school provided discipline. John Brinsley, the Puritan divine and educator, put forth the regimen. School would begin at six, with punishment for tardiness (virtually every picture of the classroom showed the master with a birch in one hand). Homework in Latin was presented and other studies pursued until nine, when there was a quarter-hour break. The work resumed until eleven, when there was a two-hour hiatus. From one to five-thirty students were again at their desks, with a quarter-hour break at three-thirty. The purpose of education was divine. "God having ordained schools of learning to be a principal means to reduce a barbarous people to civilitie' and Christianity. The challenge was to gain "the verie savage amonst them unto Jesus Christ, whether Irish or Indian . . . .' Or, Brinsley might have added, 'Child.'

The punctuality demanded of the student, the restraint needed to remain sitting almost all day at a desk would foster the self-discipline which was the object of earlier controls. As to apprenticeship it has been observed that the guilds attempted 'to instil self-discipline and respect for the social code into those for whose industrial training they were responsible.' The Shoemakers of Carlisle forbid apprentices and journeymen to play football without the consent of their masters; the Merchant Adventurers of Newcastle forbid 'daunce dice cards mum or use any musick' and inveighed against extravagant dress and long hair, even establishing a prison to jail offenders against these rules. There are instances of masters imposing fines for missing prayer, 'toying with the maids,' teaching children 'bawdy words' or even wearing 'a foul shirt on

Sunday.' Working conditions were apparently as exacting as school situations, though in the seventeenth century apprentices were protected by law.

The History of Childhood edited by Lloyd de Mause

The School Inspector

The author's father, born in 1874, describes his elementary schooldays in Pitton, a small village four miles from Salisbury where, in primitive surroundings, the education was basic and the annual visit of the inspector was an ordeal dreaded by teacher and pupils alike.

Education was a compulsory privilege that had to be paid for. The fee for labourers' children was one penny a week, for smallholder's children two pence, and for the children of better-off farmers and builders three pence. Our penny was paid by the parish. Every Monday morning after prayers all the children (except we little paupers) queued up before the teacher's desk to hand over the weekly fee. Woe to the child who had forgotten it! Back home to fetch it, straight away! No penny, no education!

The partition across the school served to separate the 'Little Room', where the infants were taught, from the 'Big Room'. When I was promoted to the Big Room I was given an exercise book – a brand-new one! This book, the only exercise book I ever had, was for copying select portions of my work on rare occasions, being for exhibition to the school inspector. Some promising pupils actually had two exercise books during their school career, but that was exceptional. For ordinary purposes we wrote on slates. In our pockets we carried a rag which, with the application of a little spittle, served to wipe the slate clean. It was also used as a handkerchief . . .

The visitation by the Inspector provided an awful and majestic end to the school year, especially a pupil's last year.

The test was not a written one but an oral examination conducted by the Inspector. Pressure on the pupils was as great as it is now when examinations loom. A child was never allowed to forget the great responsibility resting on him.

'Now, whatever thees do, thee be sure and mind to pass. I got a job looked out for thee, so don't thee *dare* come whoam and say thee's failed!'

The final weeks were filled by the time-honoured system of cramming. Knowledge was forced into unreceptive heads. Lessons were learned, parrot-like, and the cane was used liberally. The overriding necessity was that we should make a good impression when the great day came.

On the fateful morning we were dressed in our best clothes (if any), and our faces and boots were given an extra polish. At school, prayers were repeated and morning hymns sung in subdued and quavering voices, after which we awaited, in an agony of suspense, the arrival of the Inspector.

Presently a polished fly came clattering down White Way, to stop, with much jingling of harness, outside the school gate. An elderly gentleman in frock coat and top hat alighted. Only lords and rich men could afford a fly, while top hats and frock coats were as rare as Members of Parliament in Pitton. We victims were impressed and not a little scared.

The mistress opened the door and curtsied deeply as the Great Man entered. We dithering pupils also bowed or curtsied, as we did when Lady Bathurst visited, only more reverently . . . and our self-possession oozed away.

The rest of the day was a nightmare.

The Inspector glowered patronizingly and fired a question which had to be repeated several times before one girl hazarded a wrong answer. Whereat he frowned and made a note in a black book. All quaked. In the voice of the Big Bad Wolf coaxing Little Red Riding Hood, the Inspector exhorted us not to be afraid, and then shot out some more trick questions which we were too paralysed to answer. Joshua Fry, normally an intelligent boy, was asked to read aloud. He was given a travel book, which he held upside down. On this being pointed out to him, he hastily rectified his mistake and began to read: 'The skennery was rhomantic and pickcherskew . . .'

When it was time to write on our slates, we were so preoccupied in staring at the Inspector's magnetic figure and in considering the awful consequences of failure that we failed to pay much attention to the work in front of us.

Predictably, most of us failed, to the despair of the teacher and the apparent disgust of the Inspector (though perhaps his secret gratification, this being what he had expected all along).

A Victorian Village by Ralph Whitlock

Akenfield

Men who were children in Akenfield, Suffolk, at the end of the nineteenth century remembered looking forward to leaving school so they could get educated.

I walked two miles to school. There were so many children you could hardly squeeze in the room. All the same, it was very cold in the winter. Most of the boys had suits and boots on with nothing underneath. Every now and then we used to have to stand on the outside of our desks and mark-time to get our circulation back. We did left-right, left-right for about five minutes – good God, what a row we made! Later on, I heard this sound again in Gallipoli. It seemed homely and familiar. We must have been bashing some landing-stage. The school was useless. The farmers came and took boys away from it when they felt like it, the parson raided it for servants. The teacher was a respectable woman who did her best. Sometimes she would bring the *Daily Graphic* down and show us the news. I looked forward to leaving school so that I could get educated. I knew that education was in books, not in school: there were no books there. I was a child when I left but I already knew that our 'learning' was rubbish, that our food was rubbish and that I should end as rubbish if I didn't look out.

When I was six we moved to another house. It was a tied-cottage with a thatched roof and handsome beams. My father said, 'We shall be better off, boys, we shall have a nice spring of water just across the road, and that will be a great relief. Also we shall have a nice big garden with two apple trees, a Doctor Harvey and a Blenheim Orange.' We moved to this house in 1904. As soon as we got there, mother went stone-picking in the fields. She didn't have to do this because we were living in a tied-cottage but because we had to buy some new clothes. We helped her when we got back from school at five o'clock. She had to pick up twenty-four bushels of stones a day to get 2*s.* Each parish had to mend its own lanes then and the stones were used for this. A tumbril was put in the field and a line was chalked round it. When you had filled it up to the line you got the 2*s.* It would take the whole day. We did it every minute we weren't at school, and all through the holidays. It was all I can remember.

Akenfield, Portrait of an English Village by Ronald Blythe

Manchester Childhood

A deprived childhood in the last years of the nineteenth century did not prevent Sir Neville Cardus from reaching the heights of his chosen profession.

Manchester was my place of birth, in a slum. Back-to-back tenements were not unknown in the neighbourhood, but there was a Free Library round the corner, and also there were fields or, let us say, an 'open space' not yet built upon, and utilised in part for the disposal of rubbish; it was called, and called correctly, the 'Corporation tip.' In recent and more progressive years the authorities built an edifice called, with an equally nice sense of words, the 'Destructor.' During the summer cricket was played on these open spaces. Given a library and a cricket pitch, both free of charge, I was obviously blessed with good luck beyond the lot of most boys rich or poor. Here at any rate was the material I needed.

In the Manchester streets and on blasted heaths I began life, on slimy pavements in winter, in the summer when pavement and dust and grime threw back a heat as though from sunshine generated industrially. I attended what was known as a Board School, a place of darkness and inhumanity. I learned scarcely anything there, except to read and write. For four years only did I attend school, delicate years and miserable. At the age of thirteen my formal education came to an end. To this day I am incapable of coping with the most elementary of school examination papers. Any child knows more than I of mathematics (my studies in this direction got as far as arithmetic). I am ignorant of chemistry. I cannot grasp – not for long anyhow – what is a gerundial infinitive. I confuse an isthmus with an archipelago, and cannot confidently spell either. Strictly speaking, I suppose I am formally uneducated.

I earned my first money, my first wages, when I was ten years old, as a pavement artist. I have sold, as well as written for, newspapers. My parents conducted a home-laundry; or, not to be tautological, they took in washing. I once delivered the washing to the home and house of the Chairman of the Hallé Concerts Society, delivered it in a perambulator at the tradesmen's entrance. Years afterwards I dined with him one night; I was now music critic of the *Manchester Guardian*, and he wished to placate my pen on a point of musical policy. As I smoked his cigars, and drank his Liebfraumilch, I could not resist thinking to myself: 'What a world! I have delivered his washing. My grandmother ironed his dress shirts, and ironed them well, bless her. And here I am and here is he – and he is filling up my glass again, trying to make me see reason.'

I spent sixteen years of my youth mainly in books and music and in the sixpenny galleries of theatres. The men on the cricket field were mixed up with the heroes of books and plays. When I went alone on Saturday evenings to the Free Library (and my early youth was spent much alone) I did not go in the spirit of a good boy stirred upward and on by visions of an improving kind. I revelled in it all: excitement and sensuous delight. I argued with Shaw and A.B. Walkley; I went up and down with Mr. Micawber; I heard the whinny of Grane, and I saw the flames consuming Valhalla. I was Kipps, Richard Feverel and David Copperfield – in a place whose odour and atmosphere of india-rubber mats and silence of a municipal reading-room come back to me as I write. I had no time, not even when I was emerging from my teens, for the routing pleasures of my first companions. The girl did not exist in the whole world who could win my heart and passions from Beatrix Esmond; besides, I was a shy youth, except in the world of imagination, where I could be as bold as brass. For 'Book Learning' as such (to use the old term) I had no use; far different was absorption in the creations of rich minds; here was sport indeed. I could not even play cricket without aping the gods of Old Trafford and Lord's.

Autobiography by Sir Neville Cardus

Educating a Soldier's Children

With three boys to educate life was hard for the wife of a serving solider in the First World War.

All the boys got on well in Hove; they all went to the same elementary school at first, and then they passed the examinations to get to the grammar school. While this was a great joy, it was also a terrible worry. With three young boys to look after on my own I couldn't go out to work, and the separation allowance that I got at that time was very poor indeed.

It wasn't until I'd written goodness knows how many letters to the Education Authorities that I managed to get more money. But I found great difficulty in managing even so, and each time Albert got a promotion – he was eventually made up to corporal – we didn't benefit, because out of his increased money the government docked my allowance. So there was no incentive for him to try to get further.

I couldn't make the boys' clothes now. If they'd been girls I could have, but boys have got to look the same as everybody else. You can't send them to school in home-made suits.

I remember one terrible occasion, the only time in my life when I had to apply for charity. They only had one pair of shoes each and although when my husband was home he used to mend them, he had been posted overseas. I was at my wits' end as to how to get them repaired. So I went down to the Soldiers', Sailors', and Airmen's Association who sent me over to the Council. It was something too terrible for words. You need a hide like a rhinoceros, it seemed to me, to ask them for anything. Some people were used to getting all and sundry. They never turned a hair. But this was the first time I had ever asked for anything. I went in very nervous with a face as red as a beetroot. I felt like a pauper. 'Why do you want shoes for them? Why haven't they got shoes?' I said, 'They've only got one pair.' 'Why don't you get them mended?' they asked. 'I can get them mended,' I said, 'but in the meantime they won't be able to go to school. They've got no others.' After this kind of talk they returned me to the Soldiers', Sailors', and Airmen's place. I went back to them and I said, 'They said it comes under your jurisdiction,' and they said, 'It doesn't, not to supply shoes. You go back to the Council and start again.' When I went back and through the whole process again, they grudgingly gave me some forms. They don't give you money and they don't give you shoes, they give you forms to take to a special shop in Hove.

They wouldn't let you have shoes, you had to have boots, charity boots. My sons had never worn boots before. I never entered fully into how much they must have felt it. I was so obsessed with how I felt, I never investigated their feelings. Going to school wearing boots, and everyone knowing that they're charity boots because they were a special kind.

When my boys went to this grammar school, it was still a fee-paying school. So naturally the parents of the boys that were there were far better off financially than we were. A lot of them had been to preparatory schools. And they had money. Some of the boys had a pound a week for pocket money. A pound a week! I couldn't give mine a shilling.

Another terrible thing was that if you had an income of under five pounds a week you were entitled to free dinners. Well, there was no one else in any of their classes that had free dinners, and each new term the master would say, 'Stand up those who want tickets for dinners.' Well, you just imagine how you would feel if you're the only child in the class whose parents can't afford to pay for your dinners. I didn't fully understand it myself at the time. If I had realized the situation I wouldn't have been ambitious to get them to a grammar school, I really wouldn't. I used to write to the master in advance, I knew which one they would have, and say, 'Will you please not say out loud, "Who is going to have a free school dinner?".' I admit they did take notice then, and they didn't do it.

Below Stairs by Margaret Powell

The Hygiene Inspection

The weekly 'hygiene' inspection was an inevitable ordeal in the life of an elementary Bolton schoolboy in the 1930s.

On certain mornings, perhaps once or twice a week, the entire boys' senior school – ages seven to thirteen – would be kept in class lines in the playground, for what was known as 'hygiene inspection'. The demands, modest enough, were that each boy be well washed, especially round the neck and inside his ears, that his hair be clean and brushed or combed into place, that hands be clean, nails scrubbed and unbitten, that he be clean and tidy in dress, wearing either a collar or jersey – scarves not permitted – that his stockings did not hang down, and that his clogs or boots were clean and polished. Mercifully, the most obnoxious offence against hygiene, was one which passed unmentioned – being that of the unfortunate boy from a poor home who gave off a bad odour. I believe that, apart from a lack of personal washing and clean underclothes, it had much to do with living in a bug-infested house, for from such homes there was a verminous stench which seemed to attach itself to the person and his clothes. And one or two I recall were intelligent boys, but woefully withdrawn. For them there was, apart from Flash Street clinic – a visit to which would invite discredit if not odium – no agency or group concerned with or sympathetic to their plight; and there seemed no understanding of how the child himself was helpless.

There were certain boys from well-ordered homes who could fulfil all the school demands for cleanliness without a care, but they were in a minority, and there was a larger middle group that might be classed as dubious, and then there was also a bunch that might mistakenly be classed as incorrigible when in fact they were doomed, for there was no way they could escape. The working-class schoolboy such as myself (the fortunate one that is, from a relatively good home), usually possessed two shirts in all – one on and one in the wash – and after his weekly top-and-tailer at the kitchen sink, he put on his clean shirt on Saturday evening, or more likely Sunday morning for Mass, and then he wore it all the week, and slept in it every night. Indeed he hardly ever took it off except at weekends, and after a few days it was inclined to become grubby and sweat-stiffened. This stale condition did not impose itself on the wearer in the way that may be imagined, since it was the custom, and customs were not questioned. Pyjamas were almost unknown amongst the working class (they might be bought for going away at holiday time, but otherwise remain unworn); also, in winter the stone-floored homes were so cold that changing into a sleeping garment at night was an uninviting prospect. Even a good wash seemed to keep one awake.

On the Pig's Back by Bill Naughton

Corporal Punishment

It is a sad reflection on the mores of the 1930s that the inherent social and academic difficulties faced at school by children from poor homes led too often to unjustified corporal punishment.

The almost endless caning and other punishment (such as holding a boy's head under the cold water tap and scrubbing it), which would normally begin the moment official school time was signalled every morning – appeared to stem in the first place from an irreconcilable discrepancy between the set hygienic demands made by the school authority, and the inability of certain boys from poor homes to meet these; also a curriculum designed to achieve standards of education of a level certain pupils were incapable of reaching – and any breach of either meriting reprimand. Standards had to be set, but most boys were dependent on their mothers for cleanliness and appearance and for getting them off to school on time, and some unfortunate mothers seemed to have no idea of hygiene or punctuality. As for learning, many boys came from homes in which one or other parent was illiterate, some were not too sound in the head, and these homes were dingy, dark dwellings in which the adults, inured to generations of work that was menial and dirty, and sunk down as if they were in poverty and ignorance from birth to death, had little of intellectual value to pass on to their offspring; they were creatures who avoided all contact with the world of education.

These homes would usually be without watch or clock of any sort (factory buzzers and frequent calls on neighbours or passers-by served to keep the family informed), so that a boy from such a home would have no idea of how to tell the time, and would have to endure caning and abuse over being taught to read the clock. Life itself being so grim a reality to such a one, he was wholly unprepared for abstraction, and no matter how he struggled, it seemed impossible for him to grasp what the English lesson was about. Indeed, the very idea that speech had rules which needed to be learnt came as a shock to most boys, as it did to me, for a simple and familiar instrument was suddenly made complex and remote. The letter *a* had now to be recognized as the *indefinite article*, such a complex definition of a single letter did not appear to make sense. There was the adjective – the word itself was intimidating. It was a part of speech which baffled many of these boys right up to the top class, and severe were the canings which ignorance of it resulted in. Some boys had difficulty with the verb, unless it was reduced to its simplest form: The player *kicked* the ball. Certain boys looked on grammar as a guessing-game, and felt uncertain over the noun, vague about the pronoun, and bewildered by the preposition. The English lesson poisoned any desire they may have had to learn their own language.

On the Pig's Back by Bill Naughton

School Beatings

A barbarous schoolboy custom at Marlborough College in 1930 is happily now discontinued.

. . . Casual beatings brought us no disgrace,
Rather a kind of glory. In the dorm,
Comparing bruises, other boys could show
Far worse ones that the beaks and prefects made.
No, Upper School's most terrible disgrace
Involved a very different sort of pain.
Our discontents and enmities arose
Somewhere about the seventh week of term:
The holidays too far off to count the days
Till our release, the weeks behind, a blank.
'Haven't you heard?' said D. C. Wilkinson.
'Angus is to be basketed tonight.'
Why Angus . . .? Never mind. The victim's found.
Perhaps he sported coloured socks too soon,
Perhaps he smarmed his hair with scented oil,
Perhaps he was 'immoral' or a thief.
We did not mind the cause: for Angus now
The game was up. His friends deserted him,
And after his disgrace they'd stay away
For fear of being basketed themselves.
'*By* the boys, *for* the boys. The boys know best.
Leave it to them to pick the rotters out
With that rough justice decent schoolboys know.'
And at the end of term the victim left—

Never to wear an old Marlburian tie.
In quieter tones we asked in Hall that night

Neighbours to pass the marge; the piles of bread
Lay in uneaten slices with the jam.
Too thrilled to eat we raced across the court

Under the frosty stars to Upper School.
Elaborately easy at his desk
Sat Angus, glancing through *The Autocar*.
Fellows walked past him trying to make it look
As if they didn't know his coming fate,
Though the boy's body called 'Unclean! Unclean!'
And all of us felt goody-goody-good,
Nice wholesome boys who never sinned at all.
At ten to seven 'Big Fire' came marching in
Unsmiling, while the captains stayed outside
(For this was 'unofficial'). Twelve to one:
What chance had Angus? They surrounded him,
Pulled off his coat and trousers, socks and shoes
And, wretched in his shirt, they hoisted him
Into the huge waste-paper basket; then
Poured ink and treacle on his head. With ropes
They strung the basket up among the beams,
And as he soared I only saw his eyes
Look through the slats at us who watched below.
Seven. 'It's prep'. They let the basket down
And Angus struggled out. 'Left! Right! Left! Right!'
We stamped and called as, stained and pale, he strode
Down the long alley-way between the desks,
Holding his trousers, coat and pointed shoes.

Summoned by Bells by John Betjeman

The Way We Dealt
with
Crime and War

Theft

When Boswell was writing The Life of Johnson *and Gray his* 'Elegy in a Country Churchyard' *the punishment for stealing was almost invariably death.*

The period covered by the trials here recorded (1700–1780) has a very special importance. It was an age to which many people in our own day look back with longing as the age in which they would have liked to live, and it is sometimes spoken of as the 'gentle' eighteenth century. It was, of course, the age of Johnson and his circle, preserved for us in the pages of Boswell, of Gray and the famous 'Elegy', of Gibbon's *Decline and Fall*, of Sterne's *Tristram Shandy* and Henry Fielding's *Tom Jones*. But the temptation to compare past ages with our own, and to judge them by the standards of knowledge and experience we have so painfully acquired, is to be resisted. The purpose of this book is not in any sense critical or analytical. Its modest and, I think, useful purpose is to reproduce some of the criminal trials of the eighteenth century as recorded at the time, with the comments of the Editors, and thus to reveal a phase of life that is sometimes forgotten when the glories of that age are being considered. For let it be said at once that the trials here set out exhibit the criminal law in what we now regard as a barbaric and even savage state. The punishment of death was imposed almost as freely as a Magistrate now imposes a fine of forty shillings. In 1748, William York, a boy of ten, was sentenced to death, and the whole body of judges to whom the matter was referred said '. . . the sparing of this boy merely on account of his age will probably have a quite contrary tendency [to that of deterrence], and in justice to the public the law should take its course.' He was not executed in fact, the execution being postponed many times, but he was under sentence of death for nine years. Women were burnt alive in the most shocking circumstances; traitors suffered the terrible ordeal of being disembowelled; the bodies of those executed were hung about the countryside in chains; public executions at Newgate and Teyburn were carried out in the presence of great multitudes of people, when scenes of the most degrading and revolting character took place; and powerful voices still cried out for more severe and spectacular punishments.

During the period with which we are concerned, the punishment of every felony was death. It will sound quite incredible to modern ears, but that was the state of the criminal law down to the year 1826. The distinction between felonies and misdemeanours was always rather artificial, but for all felonies there was only one sentence. Grand Larceny, for example, was to steal anything of the value of more than twelve pence, and that was a felony, and the penalty was death. Privately stealing in a shop to the value of five shillings also carried the death penalty. When in the nineteenth century Sir Samuel Romilly's Bill for abolishing the death penalty for this offence had passed the House of Commons, Lord Eldon, the Lord Chancellor of George the Third and George the Fourth, not only defended and indeed eulogised this state of the law, but induced the House of Lords to reject the Bill by a majority that included seven bishops.

From the Introduction to *The Newgate Calendar (1700–1780)* edited and selected by Sir Norman Birkett

Hanging

In the early part of the nineteenth century hanging was the sentence for quite trivial offences.

When the Assizes were held on the Market-hill, of course great excitement prevailed. Hundreds of persons, residing in the Fens and the neighbouring villages, would come to Ely, anxious to 'catch a sight' of my Lord Judge, with his long wig and scarlet robes. The Court, a small one, was always crammed to excess, and the Fenmen of that day, like many of the present time, were a very unmanageable race. The crier of the Court, the javelinmen, and the constables, were unable to maintain silence; the business of the Court was frequently brought to a stand-still; barristers would sit down in despair, and his Lordship look unutterable things. At length the Judge, during the hubbub, would take his black cap, and place it upon his head. By this means silence was at once restored, our worthy Fenmen listening with bated breath to what was to follow. Then the Judge, with deep tones, a solemn and warning voice, would exclaim, 'Fenmen! disgusting representatives of Ignorance and Indecency, be quiet, and listen to me. The first person I hear speak one word I will sentence him to be immediately executed; conveyed at once from this court to the place of execution, there to be hanged by the neck until he is dead; and may the Lord have mercy upon his soul! This remarkably affecting address had a marvellous effect; profound silence would for a long time prevail in the body of the court, and business be proceeded with. 'Do you imagine (I said to my informant) that the Fenmen of that day really believed the Judge had the power to condemn them to death for talking in court?' 'Believe it? (quoth he) Yes, and I am not certain that the Judge himself was not under the impression that he did possess that power for such an offence, inasmuch as then-a-days persons were hanged for offences scarcely more serious than speaking in a Court of Justice.'

When the isle of Ely was within a jurisdiction of itself, executions took place at Ely, the gallows being situated about a mile from the city, on a dreary swamp near the Witchford road, and to which place the condemned were taken from the gaol in a cart, drawn by two horses, tandem fashion. To give exquisiteness to the culprit's feelings he was tightly bound with ropes, and made to sit on his own coffin; the executioner being in the cart just behind him. The back of the condemned was towards the horses, his face to the crowd of eager spectators, who were anxious to see the last quiverings of the criminal, now on the verge of eternity. By the alteration of the law, which took away the power of the bishop, Ely lost its judge and its gallows; but we still retain the stocks. We once had a gibbet; that, too, has disappeared. Persons convicted of great crimes committed in the county are hanged in the county town, when the law requires it.

Brief History of the City of Ely by J. H. Clements

Blockading French Ports

Life on the English ships blockading the French Channel ports in 1803 was harsh.

There was nothing perfunctory in that blockade. Seemingly so automatic and effortless, it taxed all the resources and skill of the nation that maintained it. The ships – minute by modern computation – that clung to their stations on the stormy shores of western Europe were the highest masterpieces of the constructional skill and capacity of their age. A line-of-battle ship in all her formidable glory was the equivalent in her day of a medieval cathedral or a modern Dreadnought. Her handling in the Biscay gales was as much an achievement as her making. So were her rhythm and precision in action. The perfect order and skill of the British Fleet as much transcended ordinary terrestrial accomplishment as Napoleon's leadership of his armies. Never before in human history had two such mighty Forces clashed.

The background of blockade was hard and grim. In the interstices of unceasing monotony and discomfort, there were gales out of the west that split the masts and tore the sails to tatters, and struggles with tides and rocks which had more of danger in them, wrote Collingwood, than battle once a week. 'Trice up,' ran the sea song:

> 'and lay out and take two reefs in one,
> And all in a moment this work must be done,
> Then man your head-braces, topsail-halliards and all,
> And it's hoist away topsail, as you let go and haul.'

'Fire and hard service' and unremitting toil were the lot of the men who preserved England's age-long immunity. Only the sternest duty and discipline could have kept them at their stations. They passed their lives in crowded wooden ships not much bigger than modern destroyers with three or four times as many inhabitants, and, for lack of fresh vegetables and water, suffered from recurrent scurvy and ulcers. They bade farewell to snug beds and comfortable naps at night and even taking off their clothes, and lived for months at a stretch in seclusion from the world, with nothing to gratify the mind but the hope of rendering service to their country. 'If I could but make you comprehend,' says Jane Austen's Captain Harville to Anne Elliot, 'what a man suffers when he takes a last look at his wife and children and watches the boat he has sent them off in as long as it is in sight, and then turns and says, 'God knows whether we ever meet again.' . . . If I could explain to you all this, and all that a man can bear and do, and glories to do for the sake of these treasures of his existence.' The long blockade took from men all that was pleasurable to the soul or soothing to the mind, giving them in return 'constant contest with the elements and with tempers and dispositions as boisterous and untractable.' At home their wives waited in comfortless lodgings in the fishermen's cottages of lonely Torbay, raised vegetables and flowers to send aboard in the rare, hurried hours of refitting when the Fleet was forced to stand over to its own coast, and daily made the dreary climb of Berry Head to strain their eyes for a glimpse of distant sails.

Yet the men who lived this life somehow contrived to keep cheerful and even merry. They grew mustard and cress and mignonette as Captain Markham did on the stern walk of the *Centaur*, kept ducks and pigs and enjoyed such occasional treats as little eleven-year-old Bernard Coleridge who, being invited to dinner in the wardroom, 'dined upon green peas and mutton and other good things,' washed down, since he did not relish grog, with two glasses of wine. Salt beef ten years in corn, biscuit, stinking water and brandy and maggots that tasted cold to the tooth were their more normal diet. The same lad – prototype of his race and Service – thrilled at his glimpse of the French shore and the distant, unmoving masts of Brest, played marbles on the poop with his fellow midshipmen – 'good fellows but they swear rather' – and voted the ship's biscuits; though maggoty, very good. Even when he was on the yard-arm high above the rollers or on watch at night, with his hat crammed over his ears and his cravat round his neck, thinking he would give a fortune for a warm greatcoat, he remained merry and full of spirits. 'I have got a good heart and a clear conscience, and, as the saying is, a clear heart and a light pair of breeches go through the world together.' It was a moving thing to hear the rough seamen on their Saturday nights singing 'Rule, Britannia!' or dancing on the moonlit deck with as much mirth and festivity as though they were in Wapping, even when, as sometimes happened, the rats had destroyed the bagpipes by eating the bellows. When they came home on their rare leaves, they kept the sea ports in an uproar. Haydon as a boy loved to watch Jack with his pigtail and dashing girl making high carnival in Plymouth high street and hear the hoarse voice of the fore-top-man cracking his jokes on everything that came his way – man, woman or French prisoner.

Years of Victory 1802–1812 by Sir Arthur Bryant

The Littleport Riots

Unemployment drove men to desperate measures near Ely in 1816.

A matter associated with the history of Ely. I allude to what are called the 'Littleport Riots;' and the following facts connected with them are given in Watson's history of Wisbech:-

'By the transition from war to peace, a number of persons were thrown on the country without employment; work became scarce, and wages low. The manufacturers also were much depressed, so that many discontents broke out, not only in the manufacturing districts, but in various parts of the kingdom. At Wisbech a riot was openly threatened, which was only prevented by the activity of the magistrates, and the prompt appearance of the three troops of yeomanry cavalry of Upwell, Whittlesea, and March.

'At Littleport the disorder broke out into actual riot, for on the night of the 22nd of May, 1816, a desperate mob of men assembled there, and attacked the house of the Rev. Mr. Vachell, the rector, and also a magistrate; he for some time resisted their endeavours at his door, armed with a pistol, but was overpowered by three men rushing suddenly upon and disarming him. His wife and daughters were constrained to make their escape, running nearly the whole of the way to Ely. The rioters then broke all the windows, and nearly demolished everything in the house, burning all Mr. Vachell's papers and writings, and stamping his plate under their feet; they then proceeded to different shops in the town, and to the publicans' cellars, &c., helping themselves to money and liquors, without any one daring to oppose them. Elated with their present success, they then got a waggon and a team of horses, and proceeded to Ely, taking with them every gun and other deadly weapon they could find. On their arrival at that city, they were joined by some of its refractory inhabitants, and demanded contributions from the houses and shops, besides extorting money from several persons, which was unavoidably assented to, and there was every appearance of the most serious consequences; even threats were thrown out of setting fire to the noble cathedral. The Littleport banditti, however, separated themselves, and returned to their own town, after liberating two of their confederates from prison, where they had been committed by the Ely magistrates. At length the riots were terminated, by the very spirited and active exertions of Sir Henry Bate Dudley, baronet, the Rev. Mr. Law, and the Rev. Mr. Metcalfe, the then acting magistrates, aided by a very respectable number of the gentlemen and inhabitants of Ely, and the Royston troop of volunteer cavalry, who with a small detachment of the first royal dragoons sent from Bury, proceeded in a body to Littleport; a severe struggle now ensued between them and the rioters, who had secreted themselves in different houses, armed with guns, with which they fired many shots at the military and civil power; one of the soldiers was severely wounded, whereupon the military received orders to 'fire,' and the man who had wounded the soldier was instantly shot dead, and another fell. When this took place, the rioters were completely disconcerted, and fled in every direction, but by the activity of the military and civil power, no less than seventy-three of them were immediately taken prisoners. Among them were several persons of some property and apparent respectability in life. Fifty guns and nine or ten long fowling pieces were taken from the rioters. Special Assizes were appointed to be held at Ely in the beginning of June following, when Mr. Justice Abbot and Mr. Justice Burrough were associated with Edward Christian, Esq. the Chief Justice of the isle in the commission, more than seventy prisoners having been committed for trial. The assizes lasted from the Monday until the following Saturday, when

24 were condemned, of whom five were left for execution, and the sentence of the others mitigated

6 acquitted

10 were discharged by proclamation

36 were allowed to be set at liberty on producing bail for their good
behaviour
___
76 Total
___

'After this the district was restored to perfect tranquillity.'

A Brief History of the City of Ely by J.H. Clements

Evacuation

The war-time evacuation of children from towns and cities to the country had some beneficial effects for both evacuees and hosts.

Great Britain in War-Time – XI – West Country hospitality
Probably the most notable effect of the war for the greater part of the West Country is the addition to its population which has resulted from the Government's evacuation scheme and the arrival of others who have come from more congested areas on their own initiative. Where this has led to full use being made of country houses by people who normally spend much of their time in London it has brought a welcome addition of business to local tradesmen. In this, as in every sense, evacuation may be said to be doing both sides – the usual residents and the newcomers – nothing but good, and, as the Bishop of Exeter in these columns recently quoted a London official as saying: 'The worse thing about evacuation is that one day it must come to an end.'

Meanwhile, underlining the warmth of the West Country hospitality and the pleasantness of life in the country, is the fact that Devon has been more successful than any other area in retaining children evacuated under the Government scheme, and there are still 6,400 children from London living there. Certainly these children will be sorry when evacuation comes to an end and they have to return to less healthy surroundings. Hundreds who were pale-faced when they arrived now have attractive rosy cheeks, and mothers who travelled down to Exeter from the capital by special excursion train recently were delighted to find their children looking so much fitter. They found, too, that already a Cockney accent had given way to a broad Devonshire dialect, frequently of surprising richness. On its return journey the train carried back to London only two children, and this for the good reason that their parents were moving from London to the country.

The children are enjoying life in Devon, which is scarcely surprising, for meadows, ponds, moorland and the seaside are better settings for fun and games than busy London streets or slum courts, and lambs, already about, are more exciting to watch than lorries. Also, because country air and more living room have made them healthier and stronger, they are in better shape to live life joyously. Added to this, their hosts have done all they could to make the children at home and happy.

The Times 17 February 1940